The Impact of
Teacher Leaders

The Impact of Teacher Leaders

Case Studies from the Field

Kimberly T. Strike,
Janis C. Fitzsimmons,
and Debra K. Meyer

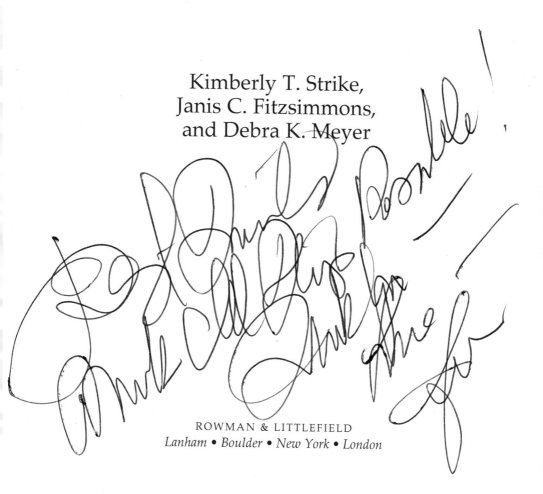

ROWMAN & LITTLEFIELD
Lanham • Boulder • New York • London

Published by Rowman & Littlefield
An imprint of The Rowman & Littlefield Publishing Group, Inc.
4501 Forbes Boulevard, Suite 200, Lanham, Maryland 20706
www.rowman.com

6 Tinworth Street, London SE11 5AL, United Kingdom

British Library Cataloguing in Publication Information Available

Library of Congress Cataloging-in-Publication Data

ISBN: 978-1-4758-2787-3 (cloth : alk. paper)
ISBN: 978-1-4758-2788-0 (pbk. : alk. paper)
ISBN: 978-1-4758-2789-7 (electronic)

∞™ The paper used in this publication meets the minimum requirements of American National Standard for Information Sciences—Permanence of Paper for Printed Library Materials, ANSI/NISO Z39.48-1992.

Contents

Foreword

When Kimberly Strike, PhD, contacted my office and offered the opportunity to write a brief foreword for *The Impact of Teacher Leaders: Case Studies from the Field,* I was intrigued. I adamantly believe in the power of teacher leadership and am honored to collaborate with teacher leaders across South Carolina in my role as assistant director at the Center for Educator Recruitment, Retention, and Advancement (CERRA). I first came to CERRA in 2008–2009 as the South Carolina Teacher of the Year. In this role, I was invited to speak to future and current teachers, business leaders, legislators, and other education stakeholders. Those who introduced me invariably used the term "teacher leader" as they described my background and my work. I inwardly cringed each time someone uttered this phrase because I was unable to make the correlation between the tasks I completed and leadership. Over the last ten years, I have witnessed educators, who had assumed both formal and informal teacher leadership roles, struggle through the same identity crisis. Current research also identified teacher leaders' inability to self-identify in this role as an ongoing challenge for the education community. It was for these reasons that it only took reading a few chapters of *The Impact of Teacher Leaders: Case Studies from the Field* for me to realize that the authors had created an essential resource.

Whether read alone or used as a companion text to the authors' first book, *Identifying and Growing Internal Leaders: A Framework for Teacher Leadership,* the included narratives provide educators with examples of effective teacher leadership. The case studies come from teachers of all levels, with different skill sets and capabilities, and demonstrate impact in different spheres of influence (school, district, and state). It is possible for educators to see themselves within the descriptions of leadership, and this connection with celebrated teacher leaders may increase the educator's likelihood of self-identifying as such. The authors also correlate the stories to specific domains and elements from their Framework for Effective Teacher Leadership. Reflective questions, which allow the reader to process what was read while encouraging self-assessment and growth in the area of teacher leadership, are included as well. Teacher leaders not only desire but require ongoing tutelage in the skills and attributes most closely aligned with successful teacher leadership practices. This book provides a vehicle to move teacher leadership practices forward.

At a time when public scrutiny of and dissatisfaction with standardized test scores, graduation rates, standards, student behavior, school report cards, and a multitude of other education topics is the norm, teacher leaders must be empowered to make the changes they believe will positively impact their students. Teacher leaders are experts in creating opportunity in the face of challenge, and *The Impact of Teacher Leaders: Case Studies from the Field* provides examples of how this can be done. This text can be used by teacher leaders, regardless of the context in which they serve, to recognize leadership, improve their own skills, and hopefully gain the courage to face the challenges before them.

Jenna Hallman, PhD
Assistant Director, CERRA

Preface

Humans are not ideally set up to understand logic;
They are ideally set up to understand stories.

—Roger C. Shank, Cognitive Scientist

In the companion to this book, *Identifying and Growing Internal Leaders: A Framework for Effective Teacher Leadership* (Strike, Fitzsimmons & Hornberger, 2019), the researcher, Dr. Strike, utilized multiple methodologies to explore teacher leadership. These methodologies included surveys, focus groups, and interviews. Through purposeful selection following data collection through focus groups and surveys, interviews were conducted as a follow-up to gain insight and more deeply explore common characteristics of effective teacher leaders. These were single instrumented case studies that were then coded to identify similarities in effective teacher leaders.

As the authors researched and searched for resources specific to case studies focused on teacher leadership, it became evident that resources were lacking. Case studies are an important tool in qualitative research, as they provide examples of implementation and examples of relationships between theory and practice; allow close examination of people and contextual situations; allow data collection and analysis, and allow for further study of people, groups, events, reasons, and questions. Case studies utilize a variety of sources and use different methods.

For the purposes of this companion publication, purposeful selection spotlighted 24 case studies where the authors interviewed teachers to collect and write narratives about their teacher leadership roles, often focusing on a specific leadership experience. All participating teachers were under a teacher contract at the time of the teacher leadership case study experience and were leading at the building or district level. Consideration in choosing teacher leaders was placed on grade level as well as geographic location. A limitation of this case study project was underrepresentation of male teachers, and some geographic locations are duplicated. However, all cases were collected from different school districts, which varied widely in their size, financial resources, and organizational structures. The authors collected the case studies using face-to-face interviews and technological platforms (Google Hangouts, Skype, or Zoom), recording and transcribing the interviews. The case study was then written up by the author and shared with the teacher leader for accuracy. The teacher leaders gave consent for publishing the case studies and were provided the opportunity to use a pseudonym and/or change the name or location of their school or district.

The Impact of Teacher Leaders: Case Studies from the Field is designed to celebrate, spotlight, teach, inspire, and encourage. First and foremost, the authors wish to celebrate the accomplishments and dedication of teacher leaders. Research clearly shows that teachers have the greatest impact on student achievement. It is also evident that teacher leaders are the bridge between their colleagues in the classrooms and administrators and parents. Initiatives can be driven, impaired, or abandoned based on the support and involvement of teacher leaders.

Teacher leadership is critical in all schools. For this reason, the authors spotlighted cases from coast to coast in the United States, along with some international examples. In an era when teacher preparation programs have decreased in number and statistics are showing that those who successfully complete those programs are not remaining in the field, it is important to spotlight the success of teachers through their leadership roles in very different school contexts.

The case studies chosen for this book are organized in such a way that they can be used as a teaching tool for individuals, small groups, or large groups. The intent is to explore, discern, and apply to one's own placement. The case studies demonstrate lattice over ladder movement within districts, evidence that education is not the stagnant field some envision it to be. In other words, one doesn't have to become an administrator to lead, and to lead with purpose and effect. The case studies shared within this text invite educators to share their journeys in an open, honest forum. Teacher leaders were open to sharing their experiences because they understand the benefit of openness and in making oneself vulnerable. Through this honesty they show their personal and professional growth.

The authors of this publication were truly inspired and honored to have teacher leaders share their stories. While each story is unique, the dedication and persistence shown in impacting their colleagues, students, and district or school are unprecedented. Many of the teacher leaders spotlighted are on regular teacher contracts and do not receive stipends or additional pay of any kind, yet their dedication to their students and community is immeasurable.

Finally, the authors encourage you, the reader, to actively celebrate teacher leaders in your community; assist administrators, school and district leadership, and school boards to be cognizant of the professional capital they have in their classrooms; and project the importance of quality teachers to our children and youth to further consider joining this noble profession.

REFERENCES

Strike, K., Fitzsimmons, J., & Hornberger, R. (2019). *Identifying and growing internal leaders: A framework for effective teacher leadership*. Lanham, MD: Rowman & Littlefield.

Acknowledgments

We would like to express our sincere appreciation to the teacher leaders who openly and without hesitation shared their stories. Through your eyes we are able to learn and grow. We thank you for stepping up to serve our children and youth, your colleagues, and your communities, most often without recognition or additional pay. We thank you for being self-motivated to explore, learn, implement, fail, and succeed. You are a true inspiration for the teaching profession.

We are grateful to our families for their unconditional love, support, and patience while we act on our innovative spirits and contribute to our field. We love you.

Introduction

Principals wanting to become instructional leaders need to believe in sharing leadership duties. This means they need to value and lean on their teacher-leaders.

—Glatthorn, Boschee, Whitehead, & Boschee (2019, p. 341)

The Impact of Teacher Leaders: Case Studies from the Field is a companion book to *Identifying and Growing Internal Leaders: A Framework for Effective Teacher Leadership* (Strike, Fitzsimmons, & Hornberger, 2019). This book contains 24 case studies showcasing teacher leadership. The central intent is to provide case studies that originated from research conducted for the companion book. Through study, exploration, and professional discussion, readers share in the analysis of data collected and reported.

To that end, the authors envision this book being utilized in several capacities to build knowledge and skills needed to exercise teacher leadership, understand foundations and identify trends of those serving as teacher leaders, and celebrate the extraordinary work done on a daily basis by teacher leaders.

Exploring the cases in this book can be done through individual analysis, small group analysis, or large group analysis; by teacher-led or student-led discussions for preservice and novice or veteran teachers; in book studies; to modify and implement practices in one's own placement; by modeling to write one's own case study; or as part of preparation for leadership programs at the graduate level. Self-assessment and reflective questions central to discussions are provided in each chapter.

The case study "attributes both theory and practice, enabling teachers and students alike to examine real-life situations under a laboratory microscope. Case studies provide a piece of controllable reality, more vivid and contextual than a textbook discussion yet more disciplines and manageable than observing or doing work in the world itself" (Glatthorn et al., 2019, p. 86; Wiggins & McTighe, 2005).

There are eight chapters in this book. Chapter 1 focuses on examination of effective teacher leadership. This chapter serves as a bridge from the companion book in that it summarizes the definition and history of teacher leadership and identifies key qualities of teacher leaders.

Chapters 2–7 focus on a specific level or area of teacher leadership. While reviewing the cases, the reader should remain open-minded, in that some of the case studies could fit into more than one chapter. Through this categorization, case study review allows identification of trends, examination of approaches, and discerning adaptations and modifications of the content to learn from and/or apply knowledge and understanding. The chapters are

Chapter 2, "Teacher Leadership in Early Childhood Education"
Chapter 3, "Teacher Leadership in Elementary Education"
Chapter 4, "Teacher Leadership in Middle Level Education"
Chapter 5, "Teacher Leadership at the High School Level"
Chapter 6, "Teacher Leadership of K–12 Specialists"
Chapter 7, "Teacher Leader on Special Assignment (TOSA)"

For the purposes of this book, early childhood spans ages three–five years, including PK and kindergarten plus grades 1–2. Elementary covers grades 3–5; middle level covers grades 6–8; and high school covers grades 9–12. The category K–12 Specialist covers those serving in noncore roles, such as music, art, physical education, special education, speech pathology, and counseling. The category Teacher on Special Assignment (TOSA) includes those functioning under a teacher contract but obtaining release time to coordinate other duties, such as school-wide assessment.

Finally, chapter 8, "Case Study Analysis," addresses how to analyze the cases and provides insight into and examples of other ways to use case studies to understand and develop teacher leadership.

To connect to the companion book, each chapter (2–7) provides specific sections of the rubric for elements of focus from *Identifying and Growing Internal Leaders: A Framework for Effective Teacher Leadership* (Strike et al., 2019) on which the reader can place each participant to practice how the framework can be used. Readers can also place themselves on this portion of the rubric based on their own reflective understanding of where they are with regard to the element(s) of focus. The Framework for Effective Teacher Leadership (Strike et al., 2019) has 4 domains:

Domain 1, Critical Competencies
Domain 2, Professional Growth of Self and Others
Domain 3, Instructional Leadership
Domain 4, Advocacy

Each domain identifies components or building blocks reflective of knowledge, skills, dispositions, and practices of effective teacher leaders. These components are further relegated to elements that provide relevant conditions or requirements of the teacher leader. Rubrics for each element are provided for the user to discern placement on the continuum. The full framework and full set of rubrics may be found in the companion book *Identifying and Growing Internal Leaders: A Framework for Effective Teacher Leadership* (Strike et al., 2019).

REFERENCES

Glatthorn, A., Boschee, F., Whitehead, B., & Boschee, B. (2019). *Curriculum leadership: Strategies for development and implementation* (5th ed.). Thousand Oaks, CA: Sage Publications, Inc.

Strike, K., Fitzsimmons, J., & Hornberger, R. (2019). *Identifying and growing internal leaders: A framework for effective teacher leadership*. Lanham, MD: Rowman & Littlefield.

Wiggins, G. & McTighe, J. (2005) *Understanding by design* (2nd ed.). Alexandria, VA: Association for Supervision and Curriculum Development ASCD.

Chapter One

Examination of Effective Teacher Leadership

According to the US Department of Education National Center for Education Statistics (2018), in fall 2016 approximately 76 million people were enrolled in American schools and colleges; 4.6 million people were employed as elementary and secondary schoolteachers or as college faculty; and professional, administrative, and support staff at educational institutions numbered 5.4 million employees (p. 53). These numbers reflected approximately 3.6 million full-time-equivalent (FTE) elementary and secondary schoolteachers engaged in classroom instruction, which is 1% lower than ten years earlier (fall 2006). Overall, total public school enrollment is expected to increase by 2% between 2016 and 2026 (p. 53).

The average salary for public schoolteachers in 2015–2016 was $58,064 in then-current dollars (i.e., not adjusted for inflation), which in constant (i.e., inflation-adjusted) dollars reflects that the average salary for teachers was 1% lower in 2015–2016 than in 1990–1991 (US Department of Education, 2018, p. 54). Statistics show that while the vast majority of teachers remain at the same school (84.3%), 8.1% move into positions in different schools and 7.7% leave the profession (p. 209). Workload, culture, and support are identified as reasons for departure (Self, 2018). However, schools and districts can improve all three of these conditions by incorporating policies and practices that support effective teacher leadership and shared decision making.

DEFINITION AND BENEFITS OF TEACHER LEADERSHIP

In our nation today we face increasingly difficult challenges of teacher shortage. In fact, teachers are leaving in numbers greater than those we are able to prepare. Drilling down, we learn that working conditions are the number one reason for resignation. While there may be many conditions under this broader umbrella, echoed in conversation after conversation is the desire to play a larger role, contribute to one's school/district in significant ways, and have a voice. Therefore, we must explore opportunities for teachers to stay in the classroom and continue to develop their craft while having the opportunity to broaden their impact on student achievement, professional development, and working conditions through participation in school, district, community, and professional decisions, actions, and initiatives (Louis, Leithwood, Wahlstrom, & Anderson, 2010).

We call that opportunity teacher leadership, and while there are differing perceptions and definitions of this term, the one that these authors advance as most accurate is: *transformative action yielding significant and sustainable results through support by teachers to teachers to improve the effectiveness of teaching and learning, and promote and influence change to improve school and student outcomes* (Strike, Fitzsimmons, & Hornberger, 2019).

This definition is a culmination of both broad and deep explorations of the concept. Common threads were identified, and verbiage was examined and carefully chosen. Following the initial development of a definition, it was brought to focus groups at Teach to Lead summits occurring from fall 2016 through summer 2017. These national summits were sponsored by the US Department of Education, Association for Supervision and Curriculum Development, and National Board for Professional Teaching. Input was provided by the participants in three areas: definition; Framework for Effective Teacher Leadership; and the roles, responsibilities, and selection criteria of teacher leaders. These data were coded and analyzed in fall 2017, and results were shared with organizations beginning in spring 2018 (Strike et al., 2019).

Doyle (2015) notes that teacher leadership provides opportunities for teachers to play a larger role in the schools, develop voice, and have an impact. Through the implementation of teacher leader career lattices, teachers have opportunities to lead from the classroom and improve at their craft, thus increasing student achievement.

Sergiovanni (2001) notes that "leaders will spend much more of their time on purposing, developing idea structures for their schools, building a *shared followership* and helping their schools become *communities of responsibility*" (p. 38). As a community of responsibility, this calls for trusted individuals who participate in decision making, are involved in others' work, and have a stake in the school's success. He notes, "Key to the success of schools with character is for their parents, students and teachers to have control over their own destinies and to have developed norms and approaches for realizing their goals" (p. 76). This is a clear reminder to develop voice to set and realize goals.

Teacher leadership provides a myriad of opportunities for teachers to remain in the classroom while exercising a variety of investments in school management and leadership, in school voice and decision making, and in understanding and implementing change that affects student learning (Danielson, 2007). Teachers are happier in such an environment and thus less likely to leave the school, district, or profession (Louis et al., 2010). As teachers continue to grow in their career trajectories and stay in the profession, teacher shortages will decrease and student learning will increase.

Sometimes referred to as *shared leadership* (Pearce & Conger, 2003), administrators who trust teachers and assure they are actively sought in decision making positively impact the school by placing those closest to the problem or initiative at the forefront to share insights. Teacher leaders are able to (a) anticipate consequences of decisions, processes, procedures, and policies; (b) enhance decisions; (c) use time efficiently; (d) avoid unnecessary expenses for materials; and (e) assist in staffing allocations.

HISTORIC OVERVIEW OF TEACHER LEADERSHIP

The concept of teacher leadership is not new. Literature dating back to the 1930s shows that teachers have long assumed leadership roles and responsibilities, whether official or unofficial, with or without recognition, formal or informal, and with or without the support of the local administration. Reviewing documentation on educational foundations, it is evident that teachers in one-room schoolhouses assumed multiple roles and responsibilities and led initiatives that impacted student learning. Regardless of the label placed on it, teacher leadership has been, and remains, part of the education system. Teacher leaders are not just one part of the system; rather, they are an *integral* part of the system, for it is often this very group of teachers who drive or rebut the internal workings of the school.

Some would argue that lack of definition has halted the evolution of teacher leadership (Strike et al., 2019). Others would argue that while there may be more than one definition, lack of consistent funding dwarfs support for either a ladder or lattice of opportunities for teacher leaders.

And so, while reference to teacher leadership persists in the literature from the 1980s through today, we have not been able to act consistently across any state, and certainly not across the nation, to systemically incorporate teacher leadership, much less reap the benefits of it that we know will have a positive impact on student learning and school and district culture and climate.

TEACHER LEADER ROLES

There are a multitude of areas under the umbrella of teacher leadership that are reliant upon the policies and culture of the district for supporting teacher leaders. Teacher leader roles, responsibilities, selection processes, criteria, acknowledgment, provision of resources and support, and evaluation vary from district to district.

Some teacher leader roles are formal (Danielson, 2007). They are announced with specific criteria and require preparation and credentialing. There is an application process for formal teacher leader roles. These roles come with specified compensation and are acknowledged in strategic plans and school board meetings.

Other teacher leader roles are informal (Danielson, 2007). In this case, teacher leaders may be self-appointed or expected to perform specific jobs in addition to teaching. Often there is no formal preparation, and the criteria for being selected are ambiguous. The criterion applied may be that you are a great teacher, you have been in a school longer than any other teacher, or something needs to be done and no one else has stepped up. Many times these informal teacher leader roles come with no compensation or acknowledgment regardless of the time and commitment needed to complete the job.

School districts also vary in the kinds of teacher leadership roles that are offered, the job descriptions, and the labels. Different titles may have similar responsibilities. Some districts utilize the label professional learning community (PLC) (Hord, 1997) facilitators, while others have lead teachers per grade level or content level chairs. In both cases, the leader facilitates team meetings of a group of teachers, often in the same grade or department, to plan for and differentiate instruction, develop innovative lessons, discuss assessment results and practices, and identify and solve common problems.

Instructional coaches in one district may do something quite different than those in another district. For example, in one district instructional coaches may provide professional development and model teaching. In another district instructional coaches may work with teachers on a plan to strengthen a particular aspect of teaching such as classroom management or questioning strategies. In some districts a teacher serves as a mentor to new teachers, and in others this responsibility is assigned to a coach.

Compensation also varies from district to district. Some districts may provide stipends for teacher leadership, while others may not. Sometimes within the same district some leadership roles receive a stipend and others do not. Similarly, in some districts teacher leaders serving as union representatives may have release time, but in others they may not. In addition to variability in compensation, the opportunities for teacher leadership also differ. Some districts view all teachers as leaders and build capacity in personnel through encouragement and targeted training. Other districts wait for teacher leaders to vocalize interest in leadership, thus relying on appointed personnel or volunteerism.

A number of organizations and initiatives have worked to raise the visibility of teacher leaders, including Teach to Lead (a federal initiative providing an opportunity for national recognition of teachers), teacher unions (i.e., National Education Association and American Federation of Teachers), National State Teacher of the Year (NSTOY), the Teacher Leader Congress (a special interest group of the American Education Research Association), and the Association of Supervision and Curriculum Development. However, one major challenge to teacher leadership remains: the inadequacy and inequity of funding for public education.

KEY QUALITIES OF EFFECTIVE TEACHER LEADERSHIP

The idea of key qualities of effective teacher leadership may vary by the group surveyed. For example, administrators may identify compliance or the ability to delegate as key qualities, whereas colleagues working with the teacher leader may be more apt to identify active listening or trust. Glatthorn, Boschee, Whitehead, and Boschee (2019) stated, "The question is not whether an individual can lead but whether he or she can lead with integrity, compassion and good judgment. Along with developing integrity, the ability to provide a supportive climate is key to the process" (p. 149).

In spring 2018, while attending "Celebrating the Noble Profession: Teaching through the Center for Success in High Needs Schools" at North Central College in Naperville, Illinois, teacher leaders were asked to create a visual that captured key qualities of effective teacher leaders. These visuals identified some common threads about teacher leader qualities: vision, collaborative, encourager, positive, and student centered. However, each group provided a different visual with different foci. One group focused on teacher leaders as superheroes who pull together pieces of a puzzle to create one cohesive, solid educational environment (see figure 1.1).

Another group created a visual with a face, where each facial feature had a specific focus, such as eye = vision. If one looks closely, there are students shown in the pupils of the eyes to capture the fact that all decisions teacher leaders make are done with a focus on the student (see figure 1.2).

These two examples illustrate how the identified qualities of teacher leaders varied depending on the group membership examining leadership. Nevertheless, both of these groups of teachers identified a teacher leader's ability to

Figure 1.1. Teacher leaders as superheroes.
Credit: Maya Adra, Katie Flessner, Laura Gonzalez, and Ashlyn Schrepfer.

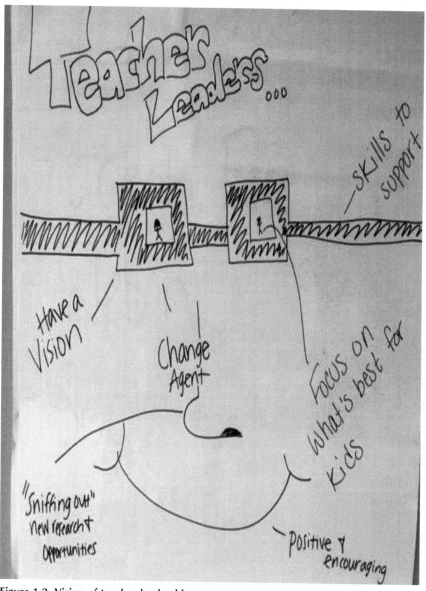

Figure 1.2. Vision of teacher leadership.
Credit: Sarah Hayes, Corinne Horner, Lily Velazquez, and Joanne Zienty.

(a) inspire others (e.g., being passionate, inspirational, positive, and encouraging); (b) facilitate change (e.g., always learning, seeking solutions and leadership in others, being a change agent, having a vision), and (c) support colleagues (e.g., being available, being collaborative, listening, admitting mistakes, coaching and mentoring, and possessing the expertise to give support).

Effective teacher leadership qualities may also be reflective of the content area or specialty of the teacher leadership role itself, such as one's work serving as a department chair of mathematics or director of special education. For example, as a department chair one's focus may be mentoring or coaching, or conducting professional development specific to department needs in mathematics. In comparison, a director of special education may need to develop qualities that focus on supporting students through transition, advocating for students, connecting with disability-related organizations, or working with families (Collins, 2018). While all of these skills represent teacher leadership, one's role determines the strategic qualities necessary to be effective.

Another determinant for teacher leader qualities and skills is the context of the school in terms of the grades the position supports:

> The role of principals and classroom teachers in curriculum planning and implementation seems to vary with the level of schooling. It is now commonplace for principals and teacher-leaders in the most effective elementary schools to take a very active role in curriculum leadership. They play the central role in articulating educational goals and curricular priorities, in influencing teacher perceptions about curricular approaches, in helping colleagues use test results, and in aligning the curriculum. At the secondary level (especially in larger schools), however, administrators are more likely to delegate these roles to department heads, whose subject matter expertise enables them to influence the curricular decision making of secondary teachers . . . Considering changes in technology and the need for curriculum alignment, teacher-leaders are now playing an ever-greater role in changing the makeup of schools. (Glatthorn et al., 2019, p. 130)

In the Framework for Effective Teacher Leadership (2019), four domains are identified to capture the crux of teacher leadership:

Domain 1, Critical Competencies
Domain 2, Professional Growth of Self and Others
Domain 3, Instructional Leadership
Domain 4, Advocacy

Each domain is broken down into components that identify skill, knowledge, and dispositions. The components are further unpacked into observable elements. Together the domains, components, and elements capture the essence of effective teacher leader qualities and provide targets for the growth and development of each teacher leader.

While specific teacher leadership roles may call for a specific focus or an emphasis on different skills based on a teacher's role, there are also similarities between roles. For example, among the common characteristics of effective teacher leaders are that they make data-based decisions and drive school-wide change.

Domain 1 of the Framework for Effective Teacher Leadership reflects the idea that there are some skills that are foundational to all teacher leader roles, while Domains 2, 3, and 4, which include professional growth, instructional leadership, and advocacy, illustrate some qualities and skills that are better developed through the opportunities provided via different roles and career pathways.

EXAMINING THE CASE STUDIES IN THIS BOOK

In the cases in this book, several components and elements are shared from each of the four domains in the Framework to provide a common lens through which to examine the teacher leader stories. Keep in mind, however, that the scope of skills or qualities being developed among these teacher leaders is much broader and better represented by the entire Framework for Effective Teacher Leadership. The differences delineated at the beginning of each chapter merely spotlight several domains, components, and elements to provide an opportunity to look closely at each case.

In reality each role a teacher leader takes on requires a broad range of skills beyond excellent teaching. Teaching expertise is foundational to teacher leadership and contingent on the leadership role and the educational context in which it takes place. This broad range of foundational and unique leadership skills and qualities allows for professional growth in multiple domains across several pathways in many educational settings.

National Board for Professional Teaching

The case studies were developed from a common set of interview questions (see the appendix). The teacher leader responses to the questions allowed the authors to develop cases to enable readers to peer into the lives of 24 different teacher leaders, the paths they have taken, the qualities they embody and aspire to, and the important work they undertake. For this opportunity to observe and learn about teacher leadership, we are forever indebted to the teacher leaders in this book.

Before considering each case, the reader may want to skim chapter 8 on the use and analysis of case studies. The case studies were written to deepen readers' reflections on their own practices, generate meaningful connections from cases to current conditions, and provide insight into the evolving roles of teacher leadership. On the other hand, they are personal accounts and as such are subjective recollections that generally cannot be verified by empirical means. Some important details may have been forgotten, and some events may be embellished. Thus, the cases should not be considered conclusive research evidence. That said, it is a worthwhile endeavor to identify commonalities and differences and to consider how each case may resemble or be different from the reader's story.

SUMMARY

In this chapter we provided an overview of teacher leadership, citing its benefits and advancing a common definition. We examined the broad spectrum of roles that teacher leaders play, both formal and informal, and we explored leadership's history, fraught with issues of agreement and funding. Finally, we examined teacher leader qualities through the lens of a new Framework for Effective Teacher Leadership that not only suggests the qualities of a teacher leader, but also outlines four domains of knowledge and skills that teacher leaders and administrators might use to guide and grow teacher leader professional development along multiple leadership pathways.

Critical to the entire discussion and not to be forgotten are the benefits of teacher leadership. Often the benefits of teacher leadership are taken for granted, and even though the concept is not new, teacher leadership is still relatively underdeveloped. Among the benefits of teacher leadership are advancement of student learning; mentoring and coaching new and veteran colleagues; creating a collaborative climate in which all voices are represented; and initiating well-informed instructional, curricular, and policy changes.

REFLECTIVE QUESTIONS AND APPLICATION

1. How do teacher leaders in your school/district community affect students, colleagues, curriculum, and instruction? What roles and responsibilities are provided by teacher leaders? What would your district/school look like without the services of teacher leaders? Are teacher leaders acknowledged and celebrated?

2. Do teacher leaders apply or volunteer, or are they "voluntold?" How are they prepared or supported for their leadership positions? How are they compensated, recognized, and supported? For some leadership positions? All?
3. How would you describe the relationship between teacher leaders and administration in areas such as trust, confidentiality, respect, and shared leadership? What policies and procedures would have to be put in place in order to advance teacher leadership and bring to capacity its benefits?
4. What state or national policies or initiatives support teacher leadership for you now? How would you like to see policies and initiatives change to advance teacher leadership?

REFERENCES

Collins, B. (2018). *Eight paths to special education teacher leadership.* Baltimore, MD: Paul H. Brookes Publishing Co., Inc.

Danielson, C. (2007, September). The many faces of leadership. *Educational Leadership, 65*(1), 14–19.

Doyle, D. (2015, February). *Leadership and lattices: New pathways across the profession.* America Institute for Research (AIR).

Glatthorn, A., Boschee, F., Whitehead, B., & Boschee, B. (2019). *Curriculum leadership: Strategies for development and implementation* (5th ed.). Thousand Oaks, CA: Sage Publications, Inc.

Hord, S. M. (1997). *Professional learning communities: Communities of continuous inquiry and improvement.* Austin, TX: Southwest Educational Development Laboratory (ED410659).

Louis, K., Leithwood, K., Wahlstrom, K., & Anderson, S. (2010, July). *Learning from leadership: Investigating the links to improved student learning.* University of Minnesota, Wallace Foundation.

Pearce, C. J., & Conger, C. (2003). *Shared leadership: Reframing the how's and why's of leadership.* Thousand Oaks, CA: Sage Publications, Inc.

Self, J. (2018, May). Classrooms in crisis: Why SC teachers are leaving in record number. In *The state.* Columbia, SC: The State Media Company.

Sergiovanni, T. (2001). *Leadership: What's in it for schools?* New York: Routledge-Falmer.

Strike, K. (2019, Spring). Broaching teacher recruitment and retention through effective leadership. In *Palmetto administrator.* Columbia: South Carolina Association of School Administrators

Strike, K., Fitzsimmons, J., & Hornberger, R. (2019). *Identifying and growing internal leaders: A framework for effective teacher leadership.* Lanham, MD: Rowman & Littlefield.

US Department of Education, National Center for Education Statistics. (2018). *Digest of education statistics, 2016* (pp. 53–54). (NCES 2017-094).

Chapter Two

Teacher Leadership in Early Childhood Education

This chapter presents four cases of early childhood educators, all preschool or kindergarten teachers, who share stories of teacher leadership. Amanda Montes shares her district-wide initiative to improve the transition from early childhood special education classrooms to kindergarten. Eleanor Peake reminds us of the importance of teaching and leading unconditionally through her leadership as head teacher in New Zealand. George Vlasis provides a unique perspective as a male kindergarten teacher and his years-long leadership in family involvement initiatives, and Alese Affatato shares her teacher leadership in the Chicago public schools and teaching preservice teachers.

Case studies in this chapter reflect many domains in the Framework for Effective Teacher Leadership (Strike, Fitzsimmons, & Hornberger, 2019). However, as you read each of these case studies, consider elements from "1b: Engages all stakeholders" (see figure 2.1) and "4a: Practices and refines resourcefulness" (see figure 2.2).

1b: Engages all stakeholders	Level of Performance			
Element	Ineffective	Initiating	Developing	Effective
Builds community through a concerted collaborative effort to reach out to disenfranchised or disengaged populations	Misses or declines the opportunity to reach disenfranchised or disengaged populations and build a community	Values community and begins to use some strategies to connect with some populations on a limited basis	Collaborates and builds community with some populations regularly	Connects with all populations to build community

Figure 2.1. Partial rubric for Framework for Effective Teacher Leadership (1b).
Copyright © Strike, Fitzsimmons, & Hornberger, 2019.

17

4a. Practices and refines resourcefulness	Level of Performance			
Element	**Ineffective**	**Initiating**	**Developing**	**Effective**
Mobilizes community resources to support student achievement, solve problems, and achieve goals	Fails to mobilize community to support student achievement, solve problems, and achieve goals	Attempts to mobilize community resources to support student achievement, solve problems, and achieve goals	Actively mobilizes community resources to support student achievement, solve problems, and achieve goals	Develops a collaborative culture to mobilize community resources to support student achievement, solve problems, and achieve goals

Figure 2.2. Partial rubric for Framework for Effective Teacher Leadership (4a).
Copyright © Strike, Fitzsimmons, & Hornberger, 2019.

As you reflect on the leadership of each early childhood educator highlighted in this chapter, consider other parts of the Framework (Strike, Fitzsimmons, & Hornberger, 2019). Read chapter 8 to further explore ways to analyze the impact of each case study. Pay close attention to the teacher leaders' decisions and the opportunities or challenges that their unique contexts afforded. Evaluate the ways in which you might have approached the situations presented in these cases or similar situations in your current teaching context.

AMANDA MONTES, EARLY CHILDHOOD SPECIAL EDUCATOR, JOHN SCHRODER EARLY CHILDHOOD CENTER, LOMBARD, ILLINOIS

"Every year we would get phone calls from the kindergarten teachers and we'd talk about how we could make the transition from EC to kindergarten better, but then we'd never put that plan in place," shared Amanda. As an early childhood special educator in a multiage preschool classroom, Amanda described a common experience for teachers: we know what change is needed, but beginning the process seems overwhelming amid all the other changes taking place in our school districts.

One of the most common reasons that teachers often wait for change to be initiated by the administration is the belief that it is only through top-down implementation that teachers will get the buy-in and resources necessary for something new to happen. Understanding the importance of early childhood transition programs and the needs of her students, Amanda Montes initiated a district-wide collaboration to create a transition program for more than 120 children.

Amanda was in her fourth year of teaching, and one of four early childhood special education (ECSE) preschool teachers in an EC–8 school district. She wanted to improve preschool-to-kindergarten teacher communications about developmental expectations for the young children—many of whom were identified as at-risk or had individualized education plans (IEPs)—as they made the annual transition from a half-day preschool program to a full-day kindergarten. Bridging the different expectations of the early childhood teachers became the focus of the collaborative efforts that Amanda organized.

Lombard Elementary School District is a growing elementary district of approximately 3,200 students located approximately 20 miles west of Chicago. The community of 44,000, which is predominantly white (72%) with a per capita income of $35,000, is changing. The school district enrollment is approximately 63% white, 16% Hispanic, 12% Asian, and 5% black, and 3% of the students represent two or more races. In addition, the Lombard Elementary School District represents student demographics that include 33% low income, 13% students with disabilities, 12% English learners, 2% homeless, and a 5% student mobility rate. The district consists of a new early childhood center, six elementary schools, and one middle school.

Like many of the surrounding school districts, the Lombard Early Childhood Program serves young children from ages three through five with identified disabilities and who are considered at-risk in a multiage classroom setting. The program's Preschool for All and Preschool Expansion programs have been recognized for excellence in inclusion by the state of Illinois with the Gold Circle of Quality Award.

At the time of this case study 120 children were being educated in eight blended classes. Each class had a maximum of 15 students, with five or six students having IEPs. A team of four ECSE teachers each taught an a.m. and p.m. class. During the first year of this case study, the new early childhood center was built. During the second year the ECSE teachers moved into the center and began the process of expanding from four preschool classrooms to seven in order to serve growing enrollment.

As one of the four ECSE teachers, Amanda had earned her English as a Second Language (ESL) endorsement with initial licensure and was in the process of earning a master's degree in teacher leadership and a second endorsement in K–3 special education when the transition project began. Her graduate coursework was an impetus for action. While completing her graduate studies and action research for her master's thesis, Amanda focused on components of successful preschool to kindergarten transition programs.

Amanda described this learning process as finding a new voice: "I never thought of myself as a teacher leader before. . . . I was the union rep[resentative], so I feel like I only had that union voice. . . . This transition project can impact everybody involved and focus on partnering with the administration." She found that her voice could change and that her passion for the project made a difference in her willingness to take risks and lead change outside her classroom.

As each new school year would begin, Amanda found that the kindergarten teachers would call the preschool teachers, asking, "What's with this student?" She believed that the informality of the communication process before and after the preschool to kindergarten transition impaired teacher collaboration. For students with IEPs, the staff held a transition team meeting at the end of the preschool year with the ECSE teacher, parents, and kindergarten teacher present. The special education facilitator for the Early Childhood Program organized these meetings, and resource teachers (e.g., speech pathologist, occupational therapist) would attend as needed.

However, as Amanda explained, "The *only* communication would happen at that meeting. This might be the first time that a [kindergarten] teacher and I got to talk." Although she found this hour-long meeting to be important, she knew that the communication and collaboration needed to be expanded. When a new school year began, Amanda used her graduate assignments to help organize a transition project. She began in her ECSE PLC meetings.

As Amanda explained, "Every year we would get these phone calls [from the kindergarten teachers] and we'd talk about how we could make this better, but then we'd never put that plan in place." This particular year she and a colleague who shared organizing the PLC meetings kept the discussion of transition planning going. Amanda also was able to connect with her elementary school principal by keeping her up-to-date on her graduate work, the transition project, and the PLC's progress. Being located in an elementary school also helped with collaboration because two kindergarten teachers were in the same building, and they were part of a district-wide kindergarten PLC with teachers at the other five schools.

Amanda began by reaching out to early childhood programs in surrounding districts to see if they had a P-K transition process, but she found that their processes were similar to her district's. She noted that this observation was supported by the research literature, which stated that only about 20% of schools had developed a formal P-K transition plan. The research literature also suggested to Amanda that the three most important components in building a successful transition plan would be (a) teacher-to-teacher collaboration and communication, (b) family engagement, and (c) a long-term process that began in preschool and continued into the kindergarten school year.

Amanda's next step was to connect with all 13 kindergarten teachers from the six elementary schools. To do this, she sent a 10-question survey to the teachers and found that all the kindergarten teachers would benefit from an organized and defined transition process for students transitioning from EC to kindergarten. Following the survey, Amanda knew she needed to get ECSE and kindergarten teachers together face-to-face. She organized four one-hour focus groups after school over a three-month period from February to April.

All 18 teachers (13 kindergarten, 1 special education, and 4 ECSE) attended the first meeting, and 11 to 12 teachers were able to attend the subsequent three meetings. At least one teacher from each elementary school, and all four ECSE teachers, attended all meetings. Amanda set the agenda for these focus groups to help the teachers align expectations in the preschool and kindergarten curriculums around four developmental areas: cognitive, social-emotional, physical, and communication.

As part of the process of aligning the standards between preschool and kindergarten, the teachers created a Kindergarten Expectations Packet with English and Spanish versions (see Lombard D44 Early Childhood Program, n.d.). This information packet was written for parents, who often seemed unaware of the differences between the half-day preschool classroom and the full-day kindergarten classroom.

Collaboration among so many teachers made the first meeting challenging. The teachers had a difficult time getting organized, so they broke up into four smaller groups of one ECSE teacher and kindergarten teachers from different elementary schools. The teachers were able to communicate more clearly, collaborate on areas of alignment, and then share their group's ideas with the larger group. Although the teachers committed to staying focused on the students' needs, there were areas of disagreement.

For example, one major disagreement involved expectations for children's motor skill development that arose during the second meeting as the teachers worked on what information was going into the Kindergarten Expectations Packet. This debate led to a discussion about the importance of classroom observations. The kindergarten teachers wanted to observe the children in their preschool classrooms, which the ECSE teachers welcomed because they wanted to show the children's progression in skill development. Similarly, the ECSE teachers wanted to see their former students in kindergarten, so they could understand those expectations better.

The next step was the organization of Kindergarten Roundtables, which incorporated the families into the transition planning process. In previous years the special education facilitator was solely responsible for running the Kindergarten Roundtables; however, during the roundtable in that year, families met with the facilitator, the ECSE teacher, and the kindergarten teacher. The roundtable lasted approximately 90 minutes during the school day (morning and afternoon session) and involved educating the families on kindergarten expectations; hopes and fears of the parents; and tips for planning a successful transition, such as reaching out to the kindergarten teacher for an early classroom walk through.

One of the important lessons learned from the roundtables was that the families were less concerned about their children's academic transition to kindergarten and more concerned about the loss of friendships, as many of the students' preschool friends would be going to kindergartens in different schools. In addition, the parents were feeling a loss of connections to other parents with whom they had built relationships over the preschool years.

Finally, as the school year ended, Kindergarten Articulation Meetings were organized by Amanda and the special education facilitator. While in previous years there had only been the formal IEP Transition Meetings, in that year all kindergarten teachers met with the ECSE teachers face-to-face to discuss each child transitioning to kindergarten. The district provided the release time for these meetings during a school improvement plan (SIP) day in May.

Each school's kindergarten team would visit with the ECSE teachers in a round robin style process to receive student folders for the next school year. The ECSE teachers would share the supports each student needed as well as the student's strengths. As an example of these needs, Amanda shared with one kindergarten colleague the benefits that one student gained from having a specific classroom job of greeter in order for that student to share a positive interaction with his classmates.

Amanda created a Social Storybook for each student transitioning to kindergarten. Kindergarten teachers shared pictures with Amanda to include in each book. This idea was the result of the Kindergarten Roundtable, at which families requested more information on the new settings and staff. The Social Storybook contained pictures of the new school, classrooms, and teachers so parents could help their child acclimate to kindergarten over the summer. At the end of the first year, two goals for the following year were set: to organize a Kindergarten Family Night and to increase teacher observations prior to and after the transition.

The second year of P-K transition planning began with a myriad of organizational changes. There was a new superintendent, a new human resources director (the former HR director had supported the use of substitute teachers for observations), and a new director of special education. In addition, the four ECSE teachers had moved to the new Early Childhood Center along with their new principal, who had previously been the special education facilitator. The logistics of the move to the new center consumed the new principal's time and made communication difficult (e.g., there was a delay in Internet services).

Amanda also noted that although moving to a new early childhood center had many advantages, it isolated the ECSE teachers. When she had contacted early childhood programs in other districts the previous year, she noticed that the other districts already had early childhood centers and transition planning seemed to be more difficult when there was physical distance between ECSE and kindergarten teachers.

The second year of transition planning and implementation built upon some of the first year's successes and introduced new ideas into the process. The kindergarten teachers were given a half-day release to visit the Early Childhood Center for observations. Kindergarten teachers who had children with IEPs transitioning into their classrooms also attended the IEP transition meetings during this half-day visit. ECSE teachers worked with the kindergarten teachers so that the IEP goals at the end of preschool became the beginning goals for kindergarten.

All kindergarten teachers were able to observe their future students in their early childhood classrooms. In addition, the social worker began observing preschool students to start planning social supports for their transition to the various elementary schools.

Although there were no after-school focus groups in year two, the Kindergarten Roundtables and Articulation Meetings continued. New to the Kindergarten Roundtable was a parent presenter who had had a child transition the previous year and explained her family's experiences with the transition process. The Kindergarten Expectations Packet and Social Storybooks were created during the roundtables and distributed to kindergarten-bound children and families (see Lombard D44 Early Childhood Program n.d. for a link to the expectations packet).

Articulation Meetings were slightly modified in year two because face-to-face meetings were not as easy to schedule. Three of the kindergarten teams met with the ECSE teachers face-to-face, as in year one. But the other three teams meet via Google Hangouts. The ECSE teachers sent the student folders in advance of the Hangout, so the kindergarten teacher could review it before the meeting was held online.

As year two in transition planning ended, Amanda noted that many of the challenges had become collaborative successes, yet she found that moving out of the elementary building made it more difficult to connect with kindergarten teachers. Amanda was able to reconnect with a kindergarten colleague at her former building, who helped survey the kindergarten teachers about the transition during a PLC meeting. The kindergarten teachers agreed that the transition process had been successful with a few exceptions, and they wanted to increase the preschool observations going into year three.

From the ECSE teacher perspective, the transition had been successful as well. As Amanda noted, the ECSE teachers received only one phone call from a kindergarten teacher about a child having difficulty making a transition, and that call was to inform them that they were adding more supports for the child. Like the kindergarten teachers, the ECSE teachers also wanted to observe their students in kindergarten more regularly.

Amanda was not finished. She believed a formal district P-K transition plan needs to be approved. She acknowledged that this was a goal for year 2 that did not happen because a new administration was busy with new roles: "I think [the goal is] continuing to become more formal and put a transition process into the district plan. My goal was to talk with the Board to get this plan in place this year, but that fell through." The district has a formal elementary-to-middle-school transition plan, and Amanda believed the time was right for the P-K transition process to be formalized.

With the move to the new Early Childhood Center behind them, a principal who was an advocate at the district level, and a new superintendent who was flexible and focused on students, Amanda thought the next year would be the right time to move ahead with formalizing the transition plan that teachers had developed. Amanda was planning to advocate for a formal working group (e.g., the early childhood center principal, a kindergarten teacher, the special education director, and herself) who could take the proposal to the school board.

Teacher-to-teacher collaboration and communication have improved, and the length of the transition process has grown. However, the family engagement component that Amanda knew was necessary for successful change has been essential to this success. Not only are parents becoming involved in the Kindergarten Roundtables at the end of preschool, but they are also strong advocates. One parent forwarded her child's social storybook to the superintendent and expressed her appreciation for Amanda going over and above to provide this important transition resource.

In April, as the second year of the transition planning was ending, a parent of a previous student Amanda taught—who was also a teacher in a neighboring district—contacted Amanda, saying, "'I was just in a staff meeting talking to my kindergarten teacher and mentioned your name because she is trying to get a transition project in place." The kindergarten teacher had learned about Amanda's action plan through her college professor. Amanda had begun this change process by asking other districts about their preschool to kindergarten transition plans, and now they were reaching out to her. Amanda's reaction was, "It all comes full circle!"

ELEANOR PEAKE, HEAD TEACHER, ELEANOR'S PLACE KINDERGARTEN, AUCKLAND, NEW ZEALAND

The vision of an Enviroschool is to inspire people to make changes for a sustainable lifestyle. Even the smallest change can make the biggest difference in the big picture of life. Interactions in Enviroschool with kindergarten children reflect Māori perspectives. It is through this bicultural approach that Eleanor Peake fosters a learning culture of love, care, and respect for diversity, oneself, each other, and our planet.

Eleanor serves as a head teacher in a kindergarten that serves ages two to five. The site is licensed to serve 40 students; however, there are 54–56 families on the roll, as students' attendance can range from two to five days (MWF, T/R, M–F). There is a waiting list.

There are six types of early learning environments throughout New Zealand. Teacher-led services include home based, hospital based, and center based. Parent-led services include kohanga reo (protects language and culture of the Māori), playgroups, and play centers. Eleanor's Place Kindergarten is a center-based public charitable plus school, meaning that all funding, income, and government support are not for profit.

The school is in an urban setting and reflects a mixed socioeconomic society, with a percentage of the community living in rental accommodations. Ethnic backgrounds in the kindergarten are New Zealand European, Chinese (both Mandarin and Cantonese speaking), Indian, and Korean. Approximately one-quarter of the students have English as an additional language.

The school is very well placed by the review board, and it received a four-year gratuity until the next visit. Compulsory attendance in New Zealand is from ages 6 to 16, so kindergarten and other early childhood education services fall within the noncompulsory sector of education. All early childhood education is *parental option*. The Māori kaupapa of whanaungatanga influences the relationship the teachers develop with whānau (families), tamariki (children), and kaiako (teachers). The teachers believe their relationships/connections are founded in forming trusting, responsive, and reciprocal relationships with people, places, and things.

In New Zealand, the head teacher is an appointed position. The person must have a minimum of five years of teaching experience. Prior leadership helps but is not specifically required. However, demonstration of leadership qualities, such as coordinating a team or coordinating families and implementation of programs, must be reflected by the individual. New Zealand grows leaders from within in an effort to sustain leadership.

Eleanor has 20 years of teaching experience and is in her ninth year as the head teacher. Duties of the head teacher include daily operations; enforcing policies and procedures of the governing association, ensuring the health and safety of staff and students, writing appraisals, mentoring, self-assessing via her own appraisal, invoices, and accounts.

. Therefore, the head teacher must be able to flip hats and distinguish between leadership vision implementation and management tasks. The role of the head teacher has an element of pastoral care in which nurturing the well-being of the whole family, the team, and children supports holistic development for all. In addition, the head teacher is responsible for daily operations, such as ensuring staff/child ratios are met and employment obligations are covered for staff, through ensuring people and environment are well resourced. The smooth running of these tasks has maximum impact on how well the team functions.

Serving as head teacher is a complex role that calls for Eleanor to constantly think on her feet. The head teacher has the duty to teach for six hours of the school day, which is contracted for 8:30 a.m. to 4:45 p.m.; however, often the role may mean working extended hours to ensure the workload is sustained from 7:30 a.m. to 6:00 p.m. Contracts are negotiated across New Zealand by a few different associations, but all teachers engage in the collective contract. There is a national retirement plan one can opt into, and the current retirement age is 65.

Eleanor's Place Kindergarten serves as one site within the Enviroschool Program. This is a national program throughout 16 regions with 228 sites in the Auckland region, and 1,046 schools across New Zealand that participate in the program. A school must be invited to participate. The purpose of the program is to integrate an environmental focus specific to the native culture into existing curriculum, thus growing environmental awareness of students, parents, and staff.

Eleanor's Place Kindergarten was invited to participate in the Enviroschool Program, and the interest of the head teacher prior to Eleanor's tenure set the stage. Specific targets of the program proved to be of interest to both staff and parents, such as sustainability of people, places, and things; cultural identification; whole-school approach; empowerment of the student; and learning for diversity. The program is ongoing, with different stages of implementation and depth. For this reason, Enviroschools show as bronze status for beginners, silver status for implemented, and gold status for sustained and in-depth environmental and systemic issues, and those who generate teaching practices receive green/gold status.

Eleanor's Place Kindergarten has participated as an Enviroschool for more than six years. The program it offers is a blend of teacher-directed goals linked to individual appraisals and child-initiated goals. This can be challenging in early childhood, as the roles are continuously moving, with children transitioning to school once they turn five years old, so adaptation and input from the teachers have been instrumental in the program's success. Thankfully the Enviroschools Program has the flexibility to be adapted as needed to work from teachers' strengths and interests. This flexibility has been instrumental to its success.

The program is not one of ticking off boxes, but rather reflective of student interests and exploration. Learning theories that have influenced team culture include, for example, Guy Claxton's (2002) four Rs: resourcefulness, resilience, reflection and reciprocity. Through the four Rs, people must exhibit they are ready, willing, and able to learn in different ways and not give up; use different learning strategies and know what to do when they get stuck; think of themselves as learners and how they might learn better; and learn with and from others as well as on their own.

As head teacher, Eleanor understands the importance of leadership theories, such as transformative, distributed, and shared leadership. As lead teacher, Eleanor recognizes the importance of teachers within her team being given the opportunity to lead. She recognizes that leadership does not reside solely with her. It's important sometimes to delegate to someone with interest, skills, and abilities. All teachers are required to contribute to the documentation of the program.

One of the projects implemented at Eleanor's Place Kindergarten focused on minimization of waste. The school focused on the change of moving to one rubbish bag per week, thus impacting the landfill. A challenge the team faces on an ongoing basis is that students are usually only in the kindergarten for two years and then move on to the primary school. Therefore, it is important that the systems for minimizing waste demonstrate robust processes, as teachers are consistently returning to the basics, due to the nature of people's changing roles.

Depth of knowledge for the adults involved grows over time; it is through this growth of knowledge that it becomes woven into the program. A strength of this program is empowered students who learn to problem solve on their own. They learn to solve conflicts in play, ascertain language used in everyday discussions, and talk about effects beyond the immediate here and now.

For example, with the focus on decreasing rubbish as a kindergartner, conversations about looking after the living environment were inspired. There is opportunity for complex and interactive teaching, as well as connections to cultural identity such as what rubbish in a landfill does to Sky Father or Earth Mother.

Assessment practices use narrative learning stories, photos, family sharing, and children's conversations to build their individual portfolios. The team collaboratively works on the portfolios. The head teacher writes stories and mentors teachers on how to write stories. Students recognize and re-spond within the stories, and the learning community uses these stories to raise the children. The topics are revisited by the children. These are called living stories.

Gardening is another area that connects students to their living world. Chil-dren and the teachers work alongside each other to maintain and discover the joys of gardening together. The curriculum integrates that of the Enviroschool so as not to be separate or extra, but encultured in the way one teaches.

As identified by Enviroschools (Toimata Foundation, 2018), outcomes for students include a sense of belonging and contribution; recognition of the different skills and qualities of themselves and others; skills of working to-gether, making decisions, planning, and taking action; increased confidence; and hands-on, practical ways to engage with the curriculum and learning.

Outcomes for Enviroschools are identified as increased pride and respon-sibility for caring for the school/kindergarten environment, more inspiring and healthy physical grounds, financial savings through saving resources, more engaged and motivated students, increased links with whanau and com-munity, and a framework and resources that support school staff (Toimata Foundation, 2018).

Outcomes for families, the wider community, and the country include trans-fer of knowledge from school/kindergarten to home; school/kindergarten and community working together; increased knowledge and experience of Māori perspectives; increased understanding of cultural diversity; and attitudes of care, responsibility, and creativity that transfer into all aspects of life as young people grow up (Toimata Foundation, 2018).

From the perspective of Eleanor as head teacher and her staff, outcomes of the program include making the students aware of language and concepts, attributes of practices from the transition point of view to continue in the pri-mary school, social-minded young citizens, supporting the idea that we can make a difference for our society and our world, and making sense of what we do and why (e.g., why do we recycle, and where does the rubbish go?).

Reflective of Howard Gardner's desire not just to describe the world but to create conditions to change it (Smith, 2002/2008), teachers advocate for meaningful opportunities to enhance and build on the children's strengths. For example, a student reflecting linguistic intelligence may be more apt to engage in and build relationships, while a child reflecting musical intel-ligence might compose a song. Both ought to be recognized as acceptable means to share what one has learned.

Eleanor and her staff understand the connection among mind, body, and spirit. The ultimate goal is guided by the vision of Te Whåriki; the New Zea-land early childhood curriculum "is underpinned by a vision for children who are competent and confident learners and communicators, healthy in mind, body and spirit, secure in their sense of belonging and in the knowledge that they make a valued contribution to society" (Ministry of Education, 2019). Eleanor and her staff view everyone as having a responsibility to look after the bigger world; it's bigger than just us as individuals.

The impact Eleanor has on her colleagues, school, and students includes the ability to build positive reciprocal relationships. Within a team, each individual member must opt to participate and be willing to do what is needed to meet the needs of the team as a whole, students, parents, and the school. Each member brings different abilities, but all agree to participate and hold each other accountable. Eleanor referred to this as "hand on heart."

The practice of supporting head (our ability to think in a reflective manner connected to best practice), heart (our ability to bring support for others and our environment/manaakitanga), and hands (our connection to practice and actions) reflects the spiritual essence of who we are, what we value, and how we reflect our values. Eleanor is cognizant of one's knowledge and affiliation of self and how that connects to both community and school culture. Through the lens of Māori perspectives, Eleanor models behaviors and encourages tamariki to make better choices and changes in their own behavior. Eleanor and her team model behavior for the kindergarten students to make better choices and changes in their own behavior.

Working with families, extended families, and teachers, Eleanor guides and supports her team to educate and advocate for their students. Understanding they have a great influence on children and their families, decisions are mindfully weighed specific to building relationships.

Working with different groups of stakeholders presents different challenges. Eleanor believes effective leaders inspire and bring people along with them to achieve common goals and aspirations. In practice this may involve working side by side with skeptical parents as they make personal shifts toward sustainable practices or exploring the worm farm with children. According to Eleanor, you excite and bring people with you.

The biggest influence on Eleanor's practice has been access to professional development in which current leadership philosophies are explored. This has built her confidence to take on a different role. A lead teacher is not a teacher anymore but does have to make the hard decisions. Team relationships are built, and how one manages is different when serving as a teacher leader and serving as management. It takes good professional development and good teaching to continue to build skills as a teacher leader.

As a head teacher/teacher leader, Eleanor believes it is vital to have a clear vision for her kindergartners' educational purpose. She likes to think of this as *vision leadership*; while this is the management side of the teacher leader, it is also vital to have a complex understanding of the team's personality dynamics so one is able to take people with one instead of dragging them along. As a teacher leader, Eleanor practices courageous conversations and has the ability to negotiate with teachers, parents, and children.

Eleanor believes having a good mentor at the beginning of a career is beneficial, as the type of mentorship received forms the teacher. Mentoring provides avenues for professional needs, such as understanding code standards and providing evidence of meeting those standards. However, as a lead teacher, Eleanor understands the importance of connecting educational theories with high-quality practice. The lead teacher requires skill and knowledge. There must be a willingness to engage others. Similar beliefs and values of team members can assist the way the team works together, shares resources, and influences the practices of self and others.

Eleanor reminds us of the importance of teaching and leading unconditionally. There is a fine balance when one gives unconditionally as a leader, as teacher wellness is central to retention, building competency, capability, and confident teachers and future leaders.

GEORGE VLASIS, KINDERGARTEN TEACHER, HOUGH ELEMENTARY SCHOOL, BARRINGTON, ILLINOIS

"We've built this network of connecting families and educating them about how to improve parent-child and home-school involvement." This case study is about a teacher's career-long goal of improving parent-child involvement through home-school partnerships. Like in many schools, George Vlasis found that although there were several family involvement opportunities, parents were not attending. At George's school there were school-wide events such as school plays and a Holiday Market after school. However, he didn't feel like there were opportunities for individual classrooms to build family partnerships outside of the school day. As he reflected on his advocacy for improving family involvement, the key for him was realizing that the missing link was teaching parents *why* these events were important for them and their children.

George Vlasis has 17 years of teaching experience: 4 years in early childhood special education and 13 in kindergarten—and a master's degree in early childhood special education. In 2015 George received the prestigious Golden Apple Award, which was initiated, unknown to him, by a family in his classroom.

George has spent his teaching career in Barrington Community Unit School District 220, located about 35 miles northwest of Chicago. The Barrington school district spreads across four counties and serves approximately

9,000 students in one high school, two middle schools, eight elementary schools, and one early childhood center. Until a few years ago, George was the only kindergarten teacher at Hough School, which is a K–5 school with approximately 300 students.

Susan Maude's (Maude et al., 2009; Maude et al., 2011) work on family partnerships is central in George's understanding of how to include families in his classroom and school. He believes that there should be no walls between families and teachers because, like with their children, having them in the classroom presents "teachable moments with the parents."

Family involvement initiatives began when George started teaching kindergarten and, to his surprise, no parents were volunteering for his classroom. So he started asking parents what their schedules were like and found they were highly routinized (e.g., get home from work, eat dinner, read books, go to bed). He realized this pattern was not optimal, explaining that "[t]hese days kids are so scheduled and they are so overbooked that they don't have a self anymore. I wanted to find a way to show parents how important it is to spend time with your child."

George began by sending articles to parents about the importance of play. George started to send games home and asking parents to play these games with their children. Some of the activities were specific to the child (e.g., share this book about dinosaurs; your child really enjoys this topic). He began slowly, wanting parents to know that these small activities could make a difference.

Then in the spring of his first year teaching kindergarten, George launched his first after-school family involvement night. He invited the families to come to school for a pajama party and invited a friend to play the guitar. As parents approached him afterward, one of the father's comments resonated. The father expressed how much he had enjoyed the event because he traveled a lot and did not get to spend a lot of time with his child.

George asked the father what he was thinking, and the father shared that he would love to come and do more in the classroom. George followed up and asked the father if he would like to start a Dad's Night with him. The father had a second child entering kindergarten the next year, so George explained how there was so much research about the important role fathers play in their children's lives, but fathers often don't find the time to spend with their children. The father said, "Let's do it!," and that began a six-year run of monthly Dad's Nights.

Each Dad's Night was planned at a different venue. The father and George began by finding out what all the dads did for their occupations and asked each to serve as an expert for a Dad's Night. For example, one father did landscaping, so on one Dad's Night they met at a local park, where he explained his job, using the park as the backdrop for his work. The children and their fathers then planted miniature gardens to take home. George found that many fathers would continue these projects with their children (e.g., planting gardens at home).

The first Dad's Night of the year would be in the classroom and the remaining eight events would be focused on expert dads. Fathers would often get back together later in the evening at a restaurant to reconnect, and they planned outings together (e.g., camping with their children). Each year a new father would share the responsibility of running Dad's Night with George.

Every Dad's Night began with a 10-minute conversation with the fathers about what the activity would be and how they might ask questions and interact with their children. As George explained, he often heard the fathers complain that all their children wanted to do was watch television or play video games: "All I would hear is All, All, All, but I was like no, it doesn't have to be that way. If you follow your child's interest or you're excited about something, you child will want to do it. Find the time."

Dad's Night became a community. The fathers took care of children whose fathers couldn't participate. But all fathers found a way to participate in some of the nights. They organized the activities so that if a father and child could not attend they would receive information about the activity and a contact parent who was willing to help with any questions.

For children who did not have a father present, any male role model for the child could come: an uncle, a neighbor, or a male figure in the child's life. Also, for many events another dad in the classroom could take his child and another kindergartner.

George was spending a lot of time out of the classroom on Dad's Night. He was often asked by his principal and colleagues if the nighttime activities made a difference in fostering classroom community and learning. Colleagues remarked that they didn't spend this much out-of-school time. But George believed it was time well spent, because not only could he see the excitement of his students both in and out of class, but he knew that he never would have been able to see the fathers' excitement.

However, George did not believe that the other teachers needed to spend this amount or type of time. He saw the Dad's Nights as a unique opportunity that probably was initiated because he was a male kindergarten teacher. And he noted that his focus on fathers had prompted some feedback from mothers about why there was only a night for fathers. But George found his motivation through the fathers: "They found that it mattered. Whenever it makes a difference—you want to do it more."

Then a second kindergarten classroom was opened and a new colleague, Jill, joined George's family involvement initiative. Jill and George changed

Dad's Night to Family Involvement Night, on which the teachers and families would go to a restaurant and make pizza or visit the local library to read and check out books.

The change to Family Involvement Night was very deliberate and well planned. Jill and George began by exploring the research, considering how the evenings could be interactive, and planning for each night to have a learning goal. The rationale for the switch needed to be well informed. For example, by involving the entire family, siblings too, the evenings could address new ideas such as conflict resolution and healthy eating.

Over a period of three years, George and Jill began with Family Involvement Night and then expanded to add a program they call Reading Around Barrington. With two kindergarten classrooms, the number of families went from 18 to 46. And families needed to buy into these activities because George noticed that when Dad's Night went away, the focus was lost too. There were only a few returning dads, and switching to a family focus needed a lot of advocacy and explanation about why the teachers were organizing these events.

In their first-year collaboration, Jill and George organized a September event, but attendance was low; only a handful of families attended. So they decided that the families needed to see the teachers' commitment first. Rather than holding another school event in October, Jill and George set up a schedule to visit each child's home and read books with families for 30 to 45 minutes. At the end of October they sent home a letter about the importance of reading and family-school connections.

Then in November Jill and George asked the families to come to school. They organized the evening like Dad's Night by beginning with a 10-minute conversation about the activity. As George explained, he knew these brief conversations were essential to the quality of the parent-child interactions during the evening. Whereas only a few families had attended the family night in September, 27 families attended in November. The takeaway, according to George, was: "We invested our time. Because families saw we gave time to them and they believe these teachers are committed."

Family Involvement Night was not a once-a-month home-school connection. Every week Jill and George sent home activities and family informational communications. They found that constant interaction supported more meaningful communications initiated by families. As George explained, "We could have conversations with families that some teachers could never have. It is not because they are not good teachers, but they haven't yet bought into families." These communications meant more to families because Jill and George were viewed as committed and trusted, and they interacted frequently in informal ways.

In their second year of collaboration, Jill and George expanded their family involvement to include Reading Around Barrington. Once a month, they organized an evening that revolved around reading. They set the dates for the year and sent out the location a week before. For example, in October they visited a spooky house in the community and used only candles, asking parents to come to the event with a spooky story to tell. During these reading nights, the teachers emphasized not only the importance of reading, but also of the parent-child interaction (e.g., they suggested that parents change the dinner routine by reading before dessert).

Family Involvement Nights and Reading Around Barrington events are now part of ongoing family-school opportunities. For example, George explained that as a kindergarten team, "We have some nights that are parents only and we talk about the social emotional, academic skills, and play skills." For George, the most important part of all parent involvement is teaching parents why their involvement with their children is important. One of the most important messages he has shared with families is how something as simple as stepping out of a nightly routine, just one evening a week, can build foundational relationship skills between parents and children.

George recognizes the time commitment to do this level of family involvement. But he doesn't believe one can do it successfully without being all in. He also believes that the family networking in kindergarten builds partnerships and supports attendance at subsequent events in the elementary school because families feel more connected. As George explained, "We see that the students are more successful in the classroom because their teachers are part of their lives and they have the shared experiences from family involvement activities."

The parent feedback across all these family involvement initiatives has been that they find their children wanting to interact with them more, following directions more readily, and showing better listening skills. The focus on quality time has paid off for families. Every new event has exceeded George's expectations. As he explained his advocacy role:

> I really wanted to find a platform where dads and families could find a safe place to build a network and find ways to work with their child in a positive way and see how brilliant their child was and give them something that everyone said they didn't have enough of, which was time. And I think allowing them to have that time to open their eyes and give them permission to say, "Hey, let's do this."

The impact on George also has been personal growth. He found that he started doing more community service because he saw the difference it made. He started volunteering more because, as he described, "I love seeing the joy and happiness in the parents and I wanted to be involved in creating that in other places." Something George thought was going to be a simple idea grew to become very powerful and formed long-lasting connections with families in ways he could never have imagined.

George sees his contribution as being the first step in his school's family partnerships, concluding, "You have to start this young. When parents are helped to make these connections with their children at a young age, you are helping children for a lifetime."

ALESE AFFATATO, KINDERGARTEN TEACHER, CHICAGO PUBLIC SCHOOLS, CHICAGO, ILLINOIS

"As a teacher in a challenging neighborhood, I always want kids to know that they have a safe place to learn, as well as that I am someone who respects them and will keep them safe. To be able to offer that supportive space and build that kind of a relationship is a really amazing experience!" Alese is a kindergarten teacher at an urban preschool through grade 6 school that is home to about 800 students. The school is 96% Latino, 96% low income, and 50% bilingual.

Alese is passionate about teaching, but she didn't start out thinking that's what she was going to do with her life. With a bachelor's degree in music and training as a classical flautist, the life of a professional musician was a difficult career path and provided little security. After wrestling with the emotional burnout of performing, investigating music therapy, and studying in Europe, she returned to the States to complete a master's degree in music and went into arts administration. It was while Alese was employed as an administrator that she began exploring the possibility of teaching and went back to school to be a teacher. "Once I got into a teacher preparation program, I knew I had *finally* made the right decision!" Alese has been teaching almost 16 years.

Alese's first teaching assignment was in second grade in a charter school in Chicago. After a year, she transferred to her current school as a first-grade teacher, where she taught for four years with the exception of one year when she answered a call to teach fourth grade. While Alese has taught several different grades, most of her time has been spent teaching kindergarten. Alese emphasized the important work early childhood teachers undertake:

What fascinates me about teaching kindergarten is the children—they're fresh and they are very honest. I'm the first to unearth this amazing treasure (child in kindergarten)—this precious miracle of a gift. As a kindergarten teacher, I get to be the person who introduces them to the beauty of the world. I am really beholding to parents and administrators who trust me with this awesome work and I really take it seriously. I am not just teaching them how to read and count, I am teaching them how to be kind friends and how to listen, how to be compassionate and how to be resilient.

In terms of teacher leadership, the formal component is the instructional leadership team (ILT), which reflects shared leadership and gets teachers more involved in the leadership of the school. Alese explained, "The ILT unpacks the messages and the instructional ideas from the principal and becomes a thought partner with the administration." Alese clarified that this kind of a new formula in leadership was being planted in a lot of Chicago Public School (CPS) buildings a decade ago and that when it started in her school, she was asked to be a part of it.

The principal invited one teacher from each grade in the building as a grade-level representative to attend ILT meetings with the principal, assistant principal, and other teachers to discuss topics important to the school. Alese shared that she had been a part of the ILT in her school under three different principals, explaining that "[t]his is where my leadership comes into play in the school. Usually, we meet weekly but sometimes bi-weekly or monthly." Past administrations had just laid down the law, and then the ILT would go back and facilitate grade-level meetings to implement it:

> However, under my current principal, who really believes in shared leadership, she just facilitates the meeting—you know sets it up and shares the tenets for the week—and she truly wants to hear from us (the teachers)—and she expects us to get feedback from the building and implement our ideas.

Alese added that it is in this ILT that the school completes its continuous improvement work plan (CIWP) and identifies the school's goals, as well as the methods and strategies they will use to accomplish the goals.

While the ILT is an important part of Alese's teacher leadership, several years ago she channeled her passion for teaching and learning in another leadership direction. Alese guided education candidates' learning experiences in her own classroom as a cooperating teacher and moved into the position of an adjunct professor, where she has the opportunity to impact candidates' thinking before they go into student teaching or the classroom. She noted that "[a] lot of my inspiration for teacher leadership comes from this experience."

"My passion for supporting teachers and education flourished with the experiences with my young candidates," said Alese. She saw the new teachers as starting out like her kindergartners, saying, "For me it is seeing that trajectory again—just like in kindergarten—seeing where young people start out—those fresh bright-eyed novices!" And she wanted to make a difference, explaining, "I just wanted to make a positive impact on them and give them the tools to make good!"

> I always strive to do as much as possible with what I've been given and that was an important message I sent my students. It really doesn't matter how much you

know, if you don't really get in there (the classroom) and teach. So experience matters! It (experience) made me the teacher I am, and I believe it is so important for young candidates.

Alese identified her strengths as being honest and always doing what she said she would do: follow through. Teachers, preservice or in-service, know that they can count on her and they, in turn, feel accountable to do their part. Alese also emphasized the importance of reflection in growing as a teacher, remarking, "We would videotape a lesson and then give each other feedback: two celebrations and a wondering." Another strength for Alese was building strong relationships with her students through humor. "Humor," said Alese, "gives everyone a chance to take a breath and that is an important ingredient in the hard work of teaching!"

As Alese talked about her teacher leadership, she explained how the leadership roles have humbled her and helped her to realize the inner workings of initiatives to change schools for the betterment of all students:

> I see now what it takes to really make a difference not only in a classroom, but in a school and a community. We have to have solid teachers and strong schools and we have to keep trying to make schools better and better for all kids! I've heard people say I am a Pitbull—I take that as a compliment. I do not give up on kids or colleagues. I'm just like a Pitbull in that regard.

When asked where she saw herself in five years, Alese identified doing more with teacher preparation or coaching novice teachers, possibly administration, and traveling. She saw her professional and personal goals as complementing each other. For Alese, "teaching is the trademark of a community. To be part of that is a great honor and a tremendous responsibility. So maybe . . . you'll see me right back here in my kindergarten classroom."

SUMMARY

Teacher leadership emerges across careers in a variety of ways and reaches different spheres of influence. As demonstrated across the case studies in this chapter, teacher leadership can represent meaningful changes between classroom teachers and families, district-wide changes in articulation across grade levels, school-wide leadership practices, and leadership that involves teaching and mentoring in teacher preparation programs. In other words, teacher leadership happens outside the classroom, yet its impact reverberates across many classrooms, schools, and beyond.

Important in many definitions of teacher leadership is the idea that teacher leadership is distinct from other types of leadership and happens outside the classroom (Wenner & Campbell, 2017). For example, Wenner and Campbell (2017) argue that a unique contribution is made when both the *teacher* and the *leader* are honored in *teacher leader*. The influences that teacher leaders experience in different spheres—their schools, their districts, their communities, and the profession—are illustrated by the chapter's four case studies.

While these early childhood educators remain actively involved in their classrooms and schools, they provided leadership across groups of stakeholders and, in three cases, across their careers. Amanda demonstrated leadership at the district level early in her career, while George's leadership in family-school partnerships evolved steadily over time. Eleanor's leadership transformed an entire school as she assumed a lead role. In comparison, Alese's leadership took two pathways: one within her school's leadership teams and another in higher education as an adjunct teacher educator and mentor.

The notion of spheres of influence is an important one in reflecting on the pathways that teacher leadership can take. Teacher leaders inspire others, and in the process they are inspired to do more and consider new possibilities. Not only do students benefit from these examples of teacher leadership, but whole communities and the profession are benefactors. As the Framework for Effective Teacher Leadership (Strike, Fitzsimmons, & Hornberger, 2019) highlights, a key component in teacher leadership is to engage all stakeholders in ways that build and mobilize communities, which each of these early childhood educators clearly exemplified.

REFLECTIVE QUESTIONS AND APPLICATION

1. Reflect on the leadership of each teacher highlighted in this chapter. Place him/her on the rubrics provided in the figures near the beginning of the chapter and justify your placement.
2. Self-assessment: reflecting on your own experiences and actions, place yourself on the rubrics provided at the beginning of this chapter. What area(s) of strength stand out, and what might you do to improve or obtain additional experience?
3. Identify the vision and purpose of the work of each teacher leader.
4. What were some of the challenges in translating each teacher leader's vision into operational terms? What alternatives or changes might you recommend? Is this something you have, or something that could work in your own setting? If not, what changes would need to be made for it to work in your own setting?

5. What contributes to each leader's success?
6. What aspects of each story resonated with you, and what did you learn from each story that might help in your own practice?
7. What observations have you made in looking at the leadership highlighted in this chapter, specific to teacher leadership at the early childhood level, compared to those shared in other chapters? Would you say teacher leadership is easier to plan and implement within the early childhood setting? Why or why not?

REFERENCES

Claxton, G. (2002). *Building learning power: Helping young people become better learners.* Bristol, UK: TLO Limited.

Education Council of Aotearoa New Zealand. (2018). *Teaching today podcast episode 2: Teacher wellbeing* [Audio podcast]. Retrieved from https://educationcouncil.org.nz/content/teaching-today-podcast-episode-2

Lombard D44 Early Childhood Program. (n.d.). *Kindergarten expectations packet.* Retrieved from https://sites.google.com/a/sd44.org/early-childhood-d44/resources

Maude, S. P., Naig Hodges, L., Brotherson, M. J., Hughes-Belding, K., Peck, N., Weigel, C., & Sharp, L. (2009). Critical reflections on working with diverse families: Culturally responsive professional development strategies for early childhood and early childhood special educators. *Multiple Voices for Ethnically Diverse Learners, 12*(1), 38–53.

Maude, S. P., Brotherson, M. J., Summers, J. A., Erwin, E. J., Palmer, S., Peck, N. F., Zheng, Y. Z., Kruse, A., Haines, S. J., & Weigel, C. J. (2011). Performance: A strategy for professional development in early childhood teacher preparation. *Journal of Early Childhood Teacher Education, 32*(4), 355–66.

Ministry of Education. (2019). *Te Whāriki.* Retrieved from https://www.education.govt.nz/early-childhood/teaching-and-learning/te-whariki/

Moorfield, J. (2018). *Māori dictionary.* Retrieved from http://maoridictionary.co.nz

Smith, M. K. (2002/2008). Howard Gardner and multiple intelligences. In *The encyclopedia of informal education.* Retrieved from http://www.infed.org/mobi/howard-gardner-multiple-intelligences-and-education

Strike, K., Fitzsimmons, J., & Hornberger, R. (2019). *Identifying and growing internal leaders: A framework for effective teacher leadership.* Lanham, MD: Rowman & Littlefield.

Toimata Foundation. (2018). *Enviroschools.* Retrieved from http://www.enviroschools.org.nz/outcomes_and_benefits

Wenner, J. A., & Campbell, T. (2017). The theoretical and empirical basis of teacher leadership: A review of the literature. *Review of Educational Research, 87*(1), 134–71.

Chapter Three

Teacher Leadership in Elementary Education

The case studies in this chapter are of four teacher leaders at the elementary level. One might ask how teacher leaders at the elementary level differ from or are similar to early childhood teacher leaders. The teacher leaders in this chapter engage in work that ranges from encouraging reading and writing to access and opportunity to engage with books, and from social and emotional well-being to financial literacy and equity in learning mathematics.

The four case studies that follow tell stories of teacher leaders ensuring the effectiveness of instructional programs. Flo enhances learning in mathematics by engaging her fifth graders in the real-world applications of financial literacy, while Addie uses local initiatives to enhance literacy learning. The teacher leader cases in this chapter also reveal important foundational skills necessary for teacher leaders to accomplish goals including trust and collaboration. Jenell builds trusting relationships to encourage her colleagues to engage in and practice therapeutic crisis intervention, while Dawn nurtures trust to engage her colleagues to collaborate and help reorganize her school's library, a task too big to complete on her own.

Case studies in this chapter reflect many domains in the Framework for Effective Teacher Leadership (Strike, Fitzsimmons, & Hornberger, 2019), but as you read each of the case studies, consider "3c: Provides an effective instructional program" (see figure 3.1) and "4c: Supports local initiatives" (see figure 3.2). In each case that follows note how the teacher leaders build trust, work well with a variety of others, and advocate for a change from the norm.

As you read each case, think about how each teacher leader advocates for something a little different to support the needs of students and how each leads, advocates, and collaborates. Note, too, that central to each of

3c: Provides an effective instructional program	Level of Performance			
Element	Ineffective	Initiating	Developing	Effective
Advocates for instruction that supports the needs for all learners	Does not advocate for instruction that supports the needs of all learners	Inconsistently advocates for instruction that supports the needs of all learners	Consistently advocates for instruction that supports the needs of all learners	Creates, implements and consistently advocates for instruction that supports the needs of all learners

Figure 3.1. Partial rubric for Framework for Effective Teacher Leadership (3c).
Copyright © Strike, Fitzsimmons & Hornberger, 2019.

4c: Supports local initiatives	Level of Performance			
Element	Ineffective	Initiating	Developing	Effective
Collaborates with stakeholders to ensure learner growth and advancement of the profession	Fails to collaborate with stakeholders to ensure learner growth and advancement of the profession	Attempts to collaborate with stakeholders to ensure learner growth and advancement of the profession	Actively collaborates with stakeholders to ensure working with learner growth and advancement of the profession	Develops a collaborative culture with stakeholders to ensure learner growth and advancement of the profession

Figure 3.2. Partial rubric for Framework for Effective Teacher Leadership (4c).
Copyright © Strike, Fitzsimmons & Hornberger, 2019.

these stories are the students and their instructional needs. Which teacher leader's style more closely resembles a style of leadership that you might employ? Why?

ADDIE SMITH, THIRD GRADE TEACHER: CHICAGO METRO AREA

While experience often is a critical precursor to teacher leader roles and responsibilities, sometimes schools, especially high-needs schools, take advantage of resourceful expertise in less-experienced teachers to advantage the children in their schools, and move initiatives forward. Such was the situation for Addie as she began teaching.

Addie teaches at an elementary school, 1 of 12 elementary schools in a suburban school district in the Metro Chicago area. In all there are 23 schools in the district and 14,659 students. The district is one of four school districts in the community and is the thirteenth largest school district in the state.

Addie's school is a Title I school with 603 students in a high-needs area where 71% of the students are low income, 71% are English learners, and 1% are homeless. There is a 7% mobility rate in Addie's district, and 13% of the students in her school have individualized education plans (IEPs). Addie's school is a larger school and hosts PK–fifth grade. "Many say the school is diverse," noted Addie, "but really it isn't as most of the students, 99% of the students, are Hispanic."

The students in Addie's class, however, are very diverse in terms of their needs and talents, just not racially or in terms of socioeconomic status (SES). Addie's students are Spanish speakers with a wide range of linguistic abilities (as reported on WIDA, the World-class Instructional Design and Assessment used with English Language Learners) and fall into the low economic status subgroup. Addie's school community is considered to be a suburb of Chicago, "but really, the community is a city and it is quite urban. So perhaps I would say the community is urban suburban—kind of a mix of suburban and urban." Within this community, Addie serves third-grade students.

Addie is in her seventh year of teaching. In Addie's first year she was in a split classroom that included third and fourth graders. Some of her students had just exited the bilingual program, where a portion of their instruction had been in Spanish, but she also had a group of students who still qualified for bilingual support but whose parents had refused placement. Her job was to serve a particular group of students identified as sheltered; these are students who are transitioning from having their instruction in core classes in bilingual Spanish developmental programs to having their instruction in English for the entire day. Addie's class then provided the context for her students' first year of having 100% of their instruction in English.

While we usually think of teacher leaders as having at least two or three years of experience prior to taking on either informal or formal roles as a teacher leader, Addie's case provides a unique perspective about teacher leadership, policy change, and need.

Addie explains that her first year of teaching was a unique time in education, as the Common Core State Standards (CCSS) were transitioning into the schools across the nation and in Illinois. In Addie's teacher preparation program, she had had to learn both the Illinois Learning Standards and the CCSS because of the context of education policy in the nation at the time. When Addie entered into her first year of teaching, she had a strong working knowledge of the Common Core English Language Arts (ELA) Standards and the Mathematics Common Core Standards, and she had developed comfort and confidence in implementing the CCSS with fidelity in her classroom instruction.

This made Addie an expert in her school, where teachers were just hearing about CCSS for the first time after years of working with the Illinois Learning Standards (ILS) and engaging in assessment that focused on the ILS. Addie explained, "I was pulled into many leadership meetings as I already had CC background knowledge, whereas teachers in my school were just receiving training."

Addie's background knowledge led administrators to pull her into professional learning communities (PLCs) as a facilitator. Her preparation also made her knowledgeable about a number of effective reading strategies that the school and district were interested in having all teachers implement, so Addie was called on to present information and ideas about working with the Daily Five (Boushey & Moser, 2006) and other reading instructional and curricular ideas. Addie's knowledge and ability to present that knowledge in practical and powerful ways led to her leading a number of task force groups and committees, as well as leading a PLC in her district.

At the end of Addie's first year, she was invited to come back to her alma mater to mentor and support preservice candidates in a special academic camp for students from her school's community and a community on the west side of Chicago "and so, my leadership experience grew."

Going into Addie's second year, it was back to the CCSS. The superintendent gave her and some teachers in her school and district some texts and wanted the CCSS curriculum to be written for ELA and math. And so, as a second-year teacher, Addie delved into curriculum development.

With that experience successfully under way, Addie was pulled into a professional team that oversaw all of the district elementary curriculum, the Elementary Curriculum Council. The Elementary Curriculum Council oversaw all of the reading and math curriculum and instruction. The district also had need for developing its social studies curriculum, and Addie, whose work was prized, was also asked to be an integral member of the team working on that curriculum project.

The school leadership experiences weren't the entire picture of Addie's professional life, however. In Addie's first year of teaching, she was told by administrators that in two years, every elementary teacher had to have an English as a Second Language (ESL) endorsement. So, at the end of Addie's first year of teaching, she began graduate classes to earn the ESL endorsement. Her work on the ESL endorsement turned into a master's degree in ESL. "That was helpful for my classroom teaching and I would say leadership, too!," noted Addie.

Addie described how many of the courses she engaged in in her graduate program focused on best practices that were evidence-based. A focus on best practices and evidence-based practices helped Addie master teaching in her classroom, as everything she was learning had application to her instruction even though it occurred outside the district. Addie explained, "The district didn't provide or require any preparation—they just had a need and I felt it was my job, so I did it."

The curriculum changed each year, and so the requirements and expectations for teachers, helping teachers, and herself changed each year. There was always a different administrator leading the pack, and usually in a different direction. Addie shared, "That was another thing I learned as an undergrad—be flexible and positive, and love learning new things." Being flexible and trying new things was a mantra that carried on into Addie's teaching and leadership. Addie explained that the administrators she worked with appreciated the qualities she developed and capitalized on them. "I always try my best to be positive, and I always try to help support students and student learning no matter what—it's my job."

As Addie began her fourth year of teaching, a new principal looking for ways to change the culture of the school was assigned to her school. Addie had just started her teacher leadership coursework, so this was an opportunity to apply some of the things she was learning. It also allowed her to try out her own ideas and fuel her own passion. Addie developed a Reading Fair with the principal and teachers at her school. The Reading Fair focused on growing and developing a passion for reading among students whose lives in school had previously focused solely on reading skills.

In this work, Addie talked and worked with a lot of community people, such as librarians, the superintendent, the director of curriculum, the director of assessment, and one of the area church's parishioners. Addie explained how the community provided bikes for the winners. She also discussed how she wanted to change the way that the community was looking at her students and school, with its stigma of low performing. Addie wanted the community to see how hard the students and teachers were working so they would see the school and students in a new way.

Addie's roles as teacher leader were primarily formal. PLC facilitator, building bilingual facilitator, and curriculum committee were all formal roles with job descriptions, applications, and stipends. The Reading Fair that Addie developed herself was informal and, interestingly, it is the project Addie identified as her very favorite.

Addie said her leadership skills have grown, but she also wants to strengthen her teaching. She feels like the leadership she took on as a teacher leader may have taken away from her teaching, though her administrators would disagree.

"Just for one year," said Addie, "I want to focus on teaching, which is a really hard job in and of itself." Addie really believes in shared leadership, and she sees the importance of engaging her colleagues in leadership endeavors, as well. Moving forward, Addie planned to focus on instruction in her classroom, but she said she would still teach in the after-school program, where she was integral in developing the curriculum with the principal.

Addie believes that all teachers are leaders in their classrooms. "They lead students after all," she said. But Addie had some additional opportunities to try some different experiences in her preservice experience that paved the way into teaching and leadership in her first year of teaching and leading and working with colleagues.

As a teacher leader, Addie always tries to keep the end in mind: the students. "I see my job as being integral with working with the principal to maximize the work we can do and accomplish together," she explained. But Addie also understands that teacher leaders have to find balance. She concluded, "I have to work on that and learn to say no sometimes, and eat, and sleep, and have fun!" Being a teacher leader has shown Addie that the sky's the limit in terms of what one can accomplish—together—teachers, leaders, parents, and students.

Addie would like to be an instructional coach, but that is not a position they have in her district. For Addie, that's a concern, as she's committed to the students and families in her district. She said, "They need me and other great teachers, too." Therefore, Addie strives to be director of curriculum or assessment, especially if she can lead from the classroom.

DAWN HAYS, ELEMENTARY EDUCATOR AND LIBRARY MEDIA SPECIALIST, INDIANAPOLIS, INDIANA

For veteran teacher leaders, their careers are a continuous journey of collaborative change. This case study focuses on a school-wide initiative to reorganize the school library in an elementary building that was in the midst of multiple changes. The case study illustrates the person-to-person relationships important when teachers lead change, and the importance of focusing on a goal. The case also highlights how every teacher's leadership is connected to the experiences before and after any one example.

After her thirteenth year as an elementary school teacher in Indianapolis, Dawn Hays took the opportunity to leave her first-grade classroom and become the school's library media specialist. This brief, three-year experience was made possible by a retirement in the school, and the fact that she had undergraduate and master's degrees in library school services and K–6 elementary education. Dawn was teaching in Wayne Township School Corporation at Mary McClelland Elementary, a K–6 building in a suburban area that was expanding. Class sizes had reached almost 30 students per classroom. The state of Indiana worked to reduce the student-teacher ratio to 18:1, resulting in seven to eight classes at each grade level.

Just prior to transitioning from classroom teacher to library media specialist in her school, Dawn found herself sharing a classroom with another teacher in a room separated by a divider. The teachers soon discovered that the divider did little to give them individual space, so they took it down and decided to team-teach, co-plan, and share the space as well as the students in more flexible ways. When the school librarian retired, Dawn took the position because of her deep love of working with young readers. As she explained, "I like to find materials on their reading level, get them interested in books, and keep feeding that excitement."

Dawn also felt the opportunity was optimal from a building leadership standpoint because she had developed relationships with all the teachers. As she reflected, there was a greater level of trust that might not have been there otherwise because she had been a classroom teacher. Dawn noticed that teachers in special areas were often looked at skeptically because classroom teachers had to be convinced that the specialists truly understood their classrooms.

In her new library position Dawn focused on relationship building through collaboration. Her approach was to provide as rich an environment of collaboration as she could: "Everything I did with them was to be helpful and supportive of what they were already doing in their classrooms." She also had to adapt to changes in her relationships with the students. No longer did she know one group of children deeply; rather she would come to know the children year after year in different ways.

Previously, the library had been structured with assigned times like music, art, and physical education. Classrooms used their scheduled weekly library time, and skills were taught in isolation during that visit and were often unrelated to classroom projects.

The move to an open library concept with no scheduled library time opened the library up to use by more teachers and students, and with greater flexibility so people could use it more often. Teachers could schedule time to bring their classes whenever they wanted, and for as long as needed. For example, Dawn would co-plan a unit on Indiana history and base what she would teach on the classroom teacher's assignment. She described it as "We're teaching together—it infused the library skills into what they were doing in the room and made it more authentic, real life."

The collaboration with teachers varied by need. Dawn still scheduled the primary grades for regular story times. Yet at the same time she would do cross-curricular work with the art, music, and physical education teachers. As Dawn explained, "The library was used in a better way and it was viewed more as the center of the school instead of just this room you go to for half an hour once a week to check out books."

The school principal and a school-wide planning committee, which included parents, also supported Dawn's open library initiative. She explained that the school principal was excited about the open library concept and wanted to see new ideas implemented. However, the real springboard was the planning committee. As Dawn explained, "I had it in my mind that that was the direction I wanted to go, but I am not a forceful person. I don't take my ideas and put them down someone's throat." She was patient and found the right opportunity.

During her first year in the library, the school corporation wanted school planning to be done by a committee with administration, teacher, and parents. The committee was charged with writing school goals. As a committee member, Dawn spent months working collaboratively with parents she already knew since their children had been in her classroom.

One of the main goals the school committee agreed upon was that they wanted to make classroom learning more reflective of the real world. As the conversation continued, Dawn saw that they were coming in her direction. She realized that her open library idea met a lot of the criteria that came up as needs for the school. Then she started talking about the open library concept and educated the group on what it could do. Everybody on the committee was excited about the concept, and the school-wide goals were written with the open library concept in mind.

Dawn's experience with various stakeholders emphasizes the ability to envision possibilities and leverage opportunities. Dawn recognized that teachers have their own ways of doing things, and some teachers want to do things the way they had always done them. She also found that some teachers were very excited: "They knew me and had worked closely with me before, so they were the first ones to collaborate." But when there were teachers who hung back, Dawn accepted that, saying, "You always have people that do that."

Dawn had promised her principal that she would make sure everyone was participating in library, and they agreed to not make being reluctant punitive in any way. Dawn began an individual teacher campaign, and described her interactions thus:

> I would go to lunch at different times and I would sit with different grade levels and when they would start talking about the units they were doing I would say, "Oh! I have some really great books that would go with your unit perfectly!" Then I would go get them. I would check them out for them and take the books

to them myself. I would find ways to make sure they did not have to go out of their way at all.

As Dawn explained, "One of my qualities is I am very enthusiastic and so I would get excited about the projects they had created themselves." When colleagues shared ideas, Dawn would encourage her colleagues, "This is so great! It is such a great idea! You could bring your students down to the library and we could . . . because it would be advantageous for both of us and the kids."

Even with all her positive support, some teachers worried about how students would approach the learning (i.e., not wanting to do the research). Dawn reassured them that she would do that part. She wanted to find ways to make learning in the library attractive and knew that if she could get their classes in once for a project, she could get them to come back to do other projects.

Key to Dawn's teacher leadership was making learning and collaboration nonthreatening. One source of intimidation was the integration of technology. While the technology was attractive to the students, it was sometimes a barrier for some teachers. Dawn would suggest how she could come alongside them, offering, "Let's figure this out together."

Within a year, Dawn felt that the library had been completely turned around. Once the teachers could see how much fun it was to teach and learn within the new design, they participated more. For some teachers it took only a semester; for others it took the entire year.

Dawn described the changes in the teachers as very individual. She did not see teachers as differing by grade level but saw her role as getting each teacher excited about using the library in a new way. She observed a ripple effect, explaining how "excited teachers found success and were happy with what they did in the library, then word would spread so it was easier to get other teachers into the library."

After three years, Dawn moved away from the Indianapolis area. At that time the school was under reconstruction and a new library space was being relocated along with the school's main office in a new addition to the building. She was able to work with the architects and interior designers on the plans, but never got the opportunity to use the new library space.

In reflecting on teacher leadership and how collaborative change happens, Dawn emphasized that education is always changing, and respect is core to a successful change:

I just really feel that respect is important. Everybody has value. Even the teacher who is older, and might be more old school and now we look at those people and assume they are dinosaurs. In reality they have a wealth of experience that young teachers don't have. We can't have that attitude. We can't even have that attitude about teachers that have a different style than we do.

Dawn explained that respect is always important and requires valuing people, appreciating their gifts and positive points. She also believes that in building respect a person must be humble. For example, Dawn described showing humility by "being able to admit I don't know everything and saying that my class is not always perfect." In addition, she explained how it is important to ask questions and ask for help, such as: "Here's a problem that I'm having trouble solving, do you have ideas? I'm at the end of my rope here, can someone help me? Can we work together to make things better?"

In addition to respect, Dawn believes that fun has to exist. She likes to say "Let's have fun. The kids need to have fun. Teachers need to have fun. Why come to work and not have fun? There needs to be some laughter." For Dawn, laughter is a powerful antidote to the stress that accompanies teaching.

Finally, Dawn believes that teacher support of each other is critical during change and that it can become lost due to accountability pressures (e.g., teacher evaluations, test scores), which make teaching more competitive than collaborative. When it comes to change, schools can throw so much change at teachers it is like drinking from a fire hose. Dawn believes that teachers have to be able to focus to do something well. When change comes, it has to be supported or the focus will be lost and it won't have a positive impact.

Dawn teaches in Lafayette, Indiana. She is a grade-level team leader and has been involved with Purdue University in projects focusing on young children's early science education. Like the school in Indianapolis where she began her career, her school is going through a change. Approximately 50% of the children are on free or reduced lunch, and they need additional supports in getting their basic needs (sleep, food) met.

Much of the collaboration that Dawn is involved in is with her grade-level team, with a focus on social-emotional learning and supports for their elementary students. For example, they have been working with community groups to implement a program in which a retiree is paired with a student as a classroom grandparent. These pairings, are designed to move with the children through the grade levels, are meant to build long-term relationships.

The leadership skills that Dawn applied and developed in the school-wide library redesign can be seen in her current grade-level team. The team actively collaborates and regularly meets to discuss their goals. They keep shared Google Docs to organize their work so when they sit down as a team, anyone can reprioritize their agenda to meet a pressing need.

In closing, Dawn described how her team of one new teacher, one early career teacher, and two veteran teachers work together. She explained that they share leadership, even rotating their meetings to different classrooms so everyone feels equal. They listen to each other and everyone shares. As she did in the open library initiative, Dawn focuses on how working together can be one of the most productive ways to address change, saying, "We're trying to think about what we can do as a team to support each other and what would make the best positive difference."

JENELL WALDRON, SPECIAL EDUCATION (SPED) TEACHER, MORRISONVILLE ELEMENTARY SCHOOL, MORRISONVILLE, NEW YORK

The number of students entering school with significant behavioral needs has increased. Therapeutic Crisis Intervention for Schools (TCIS) training provides a positive, safe approach to de-escalating students. This case study focuses on one teacher leader's call to train colleagues.

Morrisonville Elementary School is a rural school located within the Saranac Central School District in Morrisonville, New York. The school houses students in grades PK–5, with a student population of just under 400 students. The student population is 1.8% Hispanic, 97.6% white, and 0.6% other (including biracial or multiracial), and 42% of the students receive free or reduced lunch.

Jenell serves as a fourth-grade special education teacher and teacher leader at Morrisonville Elementary, where she has taught for more than six years. The fourth-grade classroom Jenell is assigned to has 22 students, of whom 6 have individualized education plans (IEPs). There are a general education teacher and a teaching assistant who have taught together for approximately 16 years.

Jenell serves as a SPED consultant teacher and team-teacher, providing and overseeing services provided to the students who qualify for SPED services (with IEPs), along with one student in another fourth-grade classroom who has a 504 requiring monitoring. The 504 is a plan developed to ensure that a child who has a disability identified under the law receives accommodations that will ensure academic success and access to the learning environment.

In the Saranac Central School District there is a mixture of formal and informal teacher leadership roles. These roles typically grow from need within a specific area, and then teachers either volunteer or are appointed. Jenell serves as a teacher leader under a teacher contract and does not receive additional pay or a stipend.

Jenell was first trained in TCIS through Cornell University in her prior district in response to a need for change. At that time, Jenell was a SPED teacher in an 8-1-1 classroom serving students with violent dispositions. Law enforcement was used for removal of students from the classroom, which was a loss of educational time for both that student and the other students in the classroom. Jenell, her chair, a psychologist, and a crisis counselor on staff discussed options to address the violence and keep students in the classroom. Jenell and the team were charged to research and identify a program, and Cornell University's TCIS program was chosen. Her chair and superintendent supported it and provided the funding necessary.

The original training proved to be intense and required an immense amount of work throughout the five days of training. Jenell was trained along with a crisis counselor and psychologist. The training proved valuable but was more for individual professional training with impact on one's own small environment, without the expectation to share the training with others in its beginning stages within the district.

Then Jenell moved to her current district, where one psychologist was trained in TCIS. The SPED coordinator was open-minded, and an additional psychologist and two SPED teachers were trained, for a total of five district-wide. These five trainers provide training in groups of 20 with two trainers per group. TCIS originally focused on residential needs, so anyone can be trained. The neediest populations were the focus at the start. Seven years later, approximately 70% of the district faculty, staff, and personnel were trained in TCIS. The intended outcomes of training personnel in TCIS were to:

1. Keep students within the classroom setting. Older programs focused on removal of students engaging in inappropriate behaviors; however, these are being eliminated in an effort to keep students in, and engaged in, the classroom.
2. Teach de-escalation techniques to the faculty and staff.
3. Decrease the number of office referrals and calls to the office.

These outcomes were not legislation driven, but rather identified in an effort to provide and promote a safe, productive, and successful educational experience.

Some challenges that had to be overcome were related to some of the teachers not being on board with the TCIS techniques. Some expressed concern that there was too much listening or talking things out with the child. Others expressed an apprehension about placing their hands on a child, even with documented training. Understanding there would be less impact if personnel were reluctant, Jenell and others provided a comprehensive presentation to the school board. In response, the school board created policies for TCIS-trained personnel and appropriate interactions with a student. This provided peace of mind for some personnel, while others still opted not to proceed with the hands-on approach. These teachers are considered partially trained.

Another challenge has been the time and resources it takes to conduct TCIS training. While the original training at Cornell was five days long, Jenell has brought it down to four days. This requires substitute teachers for 20 trainees and two trainers. Teachers often don't like to be out of their classrooms for that length of time. In addition, TCIS is focused on addressing a crisis, not on poor classroom management. Therefore, its success depends largely on effective daily classroom management by the classroom teacher.

Success has been documented through a significant decrease in office discipline referrals (ODR), specifically those reflecting major behavioral issues. There has been a positive impact for all. Trainers ascertain that TCIS training proactively prevents or de-escalates potential crisis situations with students; manages a crisis situation in a therapeutic manner, and if necessary, intervenes physically in a manner that reduces the risk of harm to students and staff; and processes the crisis event with students to help improve their coping strategies and allows staff to meet with the student to develop a plan to appropriately deal with the behavior. But the teaching population had to buy in to produce these results.

This buy-in is precisely what has happened at Morrisonville Elementary, with the PK–5 staff working closely together and collaborating. The faculty, staff, and leadership recognize that if they didn't have TCIS, students would probably be in an alternative setting. The open-mindedness of the teachers has proven productive through professional conversation, monthly meetings, ongoing training, review of strategies, and focus on specific students. In partnership, parents often seek counsel and request techniques that work with their children.

As a teacher leader, Jenell works two jobs: as a fourth-grade SPED teacher and a TCIS trainer. This dual position can be challenging, because Jenell's training commitment pulls her from the classroom at times. The time out of the classroom is contingent on the number of personnel who need to be trained, need for recertification, and effective application of the training provided. It can be difficult to manage both positions, which in addition to the extended days can prove to be very time-consuming. Duties associated with the training are preparation, planning and execution of the training, documentation and maintaining accurate files of training records, recertification for all trained personnel each year, and recertification as a trainer every two years.

As Jenell reflected on her teacher leadership, she recalled her preparation for this role. She realized she had been ready for something new and recognized that what she was doing in her classroom with a challenging group of students was not working. She knew she wanted to make a difference and researched possibilities. Her research led her to Cornell University's TCIS program, and her chair and superintendent supported her and provided necessary resources (i.e., time, training, and finances).

Although the training proved to be an extreme amount of work, the results have exceeded expectations. With 10 years of experience prior to the original training, Jenell recognized the importance of the program, and became a teacher leader—a trainer.

Jenell recognizes her strengths as being flexible, approachable, accessible, calm, laid-back, and informative. She tells those she's training to relax and they will learn together. As she has trained throughout the years, she has gained confidence. Her biggest challenge is managing her regular teaching job along with the additional role of TCIS trainer. She continues to balance the best use of time.

Jenell recognizes that her TCIS training and teacher leadership role have allowed her to step back and look at students as individuals rather than a class. The old adage *fair for one is not always fair for the other* highlights the understanding that students are individuals. Through her teacher leadership, Jenell sees benefits in training anyone interested in TCIS and the positive impact it has on students. Jenell enjoys listening to success stories and being approached by colleagues searching for approaches to improving student behavior. Leadership has recognized the impact of the program with teachers taking a different approach and being successful with it.

Janell is willing to explore the possibility of an administrative role, or perhaps a permanent TCIS training position through Cornell University. With 17 years of experience, this teacher leader is expanding her options.

FLORENCE FALATKO, FIFTH-GRADE TEACHER, CROMWELL VALLEY MAGNET SCHOOL, BALTIMORE COUNTY, MARYLAND

Students are often reluctant learners when it comes to mathematics, but the teacher leader in this case brings mathematics into the real world as she advocates for financial literacy and engages students and her colleagues in the stock market!

Florence, better known as Flo by her colleagues, is a fifth-grade math teacher in Baltimore County Public Schools at Cromwell Valley Magnet Elementary School in Towson, Maryland. It is a STEAM magnet school. There are 370 students in Flo's K–5 school, and the average class size is 24 students. Flo described the school as very diverse. Thirty-five percent of the students are children of color. Because it is a magnet school, parents from all over the county apply for their children to attend the school when they are in kindergarten through second grade, and the children are then selected through a lottery system. If a child is selected and has an older sibling, the older sibling may attend, too, if there is an opening.

Flo described herself as a career changer. For her first degree, Flo majored in economics, then managed a hedge fund and obtained her chartered financial analyst designation. She took time off to raise a family, and it was during the time she was raising her two sons that she discovered teaching. Flo explained that she volunteered at her sons' school and that it was the principal who told her she ought to be a teacher.

Grounded by her parenting and volunteer experience and with encouragement from her children's principal, Flo returned to school and entered a rigorous master of art in teaching (MAT) program at Towson University. She describes the program as an intense yearlong boot camp that required not only her commitment and dedication but also her family's. Flo explained that the program began in May and was a full-time commitment.

Flo explained that her work to complete the MAT was challenging for her and for her family, but she added, "I was used to persisting. As a young student myself, I was raised in a single parent family by my mom. I struggled with math, but I was enthralled with math's problem-solving nature and even when my teachers said I should go in another direction. I continued through high school and into economics."

Upon completion of her MAT, Flo began interviewing for jobs. "I was lucky to interview with Cromwell and was offered a position." Even though Flo was told that there was more of a commitment to time at Cromwell, as it was a magnet school, she accepted. Flo explained, "We have lots of after school and evening programs—coding and robotics, and the like . . . and you have to commit to all of it. That's the principal's message to all of the candidates that are interviewed." Flo was delighted to have this challenge, as she knew that she would learn a great deal being at a magnet school like this.

Flo started teaching fourth-grade social studies and science. It was about three years later that the principal said, "You should be teaching math!" And Flo heartily agreed.

"I think it's important to find out what drives you as a teacher—what you are passionate about." Flo talks to her students about finding their passion. "One student said they thought I was passionate about teaching—another said—yeah—but she is really passionate about financial literacy." The mistakes that were made when I was a student impacted who I am, explained Flo. Flo said that part of her passion is fired by her own educational experiences and the doors people tried to close on her. Flo believes that teachers should never close doors. "I equate it to Field of Dreams—never underestimate, rather build it and they will come." Flo went on to say that she sees there are many avenues of learning. "My passion grew from my mistakes and the mistakes that were made with me."

Flo shared her story. "I grew up in a single family home where we pulled bills out of a bowl to decide who would get paid that month." Flo continued to explain that when she started college, she saw kiosks at school everywhere that were giving out credit cards. To Flo that indicated, "I could buy anything I wanted." Because Flo didn't understand how credit cards worked, she used them and went into debt. When Flo started teaching math at Cromwell, she found there was a natural infusion of finance in math, and she knew that integrating math and finance would work for the students in her classes.

That was the beginning of Flo's infusing financial literacy, and financial literacy became a drum that Flo started beating. Flo finally got permission to start a Stock Market Club before school. "Fifty-six out of seventy students eligible were coming and I learned that the reason some weren't coming was because of no transportation." Flo thought that it wasn't equitable for some students to be able to take advantage of the club and others to be denied because of transportation. Flo was convinced that the school should offer the stock club experience to all of the children.

Flo went on to explain that she ran her class like a classroom economy: "Everyone applies for a job." She explained that in her classroom community she has such jobs as social worker and climate specialist, social media specialist, tweeter, and photographer. Flo explained that the students receive fake money and have access to banking and spending their money. "Behavior is not a problem," explained Flo, "as this (classroom) is their community."

Along the way, Flo received significant awards such as the Financial Capability Award for Teaching in Maryland. Flo explained that this award brought the local press out. Flo also had a student who was a national winner in SIFMA's Stock Market InvestWrite® competition. Flo was chosen to be a Maryland master teacher of financial literacy and was given the opportunity to travel around the state to teach financial literacy. This visibility prompted Flo's principal to get excited about the Stock Market Game and implement it in all the fifth-grade math classes.

Flo presented her ideas and work at a variety of conferences. As a result, they are taking root. Flo explained, "I wrote for the Baltimore County Education Foundation grant and received one of the grants." Flo called the program Ignite Financial Literacy. She wrote lessons and units for kindergarten through fifth grade and then started having parent nights on financial literacy.

While there were many presenters, the highlight of the evening was when her fifth graders presented their stock portfolios and told everyone what they should know about stocks. Flo described the response: "The county superintendent came and said 'why isn't this happening in all the schools?'" Flo also had an alumnus in high school come and speak. He said that because he did the Stock Market Game in fifth grade, he wasn't afraid of stocks.

Flo's superintendent said, "We need this throughout the county!" And Flo was awarded the Presidential Award for Excellence in Mathematics and Science. This went out in the news, and suddenly Flo had an even bigger voice. That is how Flo began working with the county social studies department. In the summer of 2017, Flo wrote the middle school curriculum for the county. Now she is writing curriculum for K–5.

Additional awards and grants allowed Flo to begin both a Girls in Finance Club and a Boys in Finance Club. And Flo has an annual parent Financial Literacy Night, on which the children go to the cafeteria and engage in projects while parents are learning. The audience for Financial Literacy Night also includes legislators. Throughout all this Flo has been working with the Maryland Council on Economic Education. "We are doing a Women in Finance Day. This will be like a speed dating where girls go from table to table to learn about what women are doing in the finance world."

"I had math anxiety my whole life, so I get the whole math anxiety issue with kids," expounded Flo. In 2018, Flo was in her sixteenth year of teaching both advanced and regular math for fifth graders, and she was also doing a lot of research on equity and math. "I've learned a lot in this work," stated Flo. Flo learned that many of the assessments and curricula used in mathematics are inequitable. She explained that this inequity isn't intentional, but that the assessments and curriculum are written for white privilege. "I've been working on meeting students' needs and finding their interests. I want to know what drives students and their interest in math."

"On top of that," said Flo, "I've infused them (my students) with a financial literacy program." Flo is working with the county to incorporate financial literacy county-wide. Though financial literacy is something unique at Flo's school, Flo hopes that eventually everyone will have financial literacy so that future generations don't make the mistakes that our generation made. Flo added, "I am still trying to grow ideas about equity, but the kinds of programs I've developed help." She dreams that these programs and ideas will take off throughout the state.

Flo also takes her students to Towson University, where they visit the finance department, get a tour of the campus, and even get to see a dining hall. The day concludes with going to a college event like a basketball game. "The impact is huge!" exclaimed Flo. "One student queried, 'Is this what college is like?' I said, 'Yes, but it is also a lot of work, too.'" Flo explained that for this student the experience was really a turnaround: "There's so much growth and so much excitement in watching students learn and grow. I'm just thrilled to be a little part of this."

Flo talked about the idea that for some teachers there is an element that financial literacy is just one more thing to add to an already busy schedule, but Flo shared, "I think the biggest impact hasn't been what I've been doing but what the students are doing. Their achievement is on the rise."

Flo's students explain tough concepts in terms of the stock game and the classroom economy. They analyze stocks and use ratios and can explain some tough ideas, and they have relatively sophisticated perspectives. Flo's students go and mentor younger students and do team projects. Flo reads trade books to them and then her students take over. "And they are ten!" exclaimed Flo.

"Other teachers," Flo added, "see the importance of financial literacy because they see what my students can do. I used to hear that's Flo's thing, but not anymore." Flo continued that many teachers feel they don't know enough about finance, so she has a teacher financial time when just teachers come into her classroom and talk. Nothing formal—just a drop in and talk to her.

"It's been really fun!" Flo said they aren't managing a portfolio together but offered that maybe that will come. Like any field, there's so much change in the world of finance and she explained that it's like anything: you don't know everything when you first teach it; you don't have to be the sage on the stage.

> The lesson I've learned and the message that I give to teachers wherever I go is, find your passion. For me it is financial literacy—it's what drives me to find new ways to teach and it makes teaching and learning fun for me and my students.

For Flo, teacher leadership is formalized in the sense that she's been asked to work with the county social studies department. "But," countered Flo, "I don't have a title, I just go out and facilitate learning just like all teachers go out and facilitate learning with the student in their classroom." For Flo teacher leadership has been a wonderful learning process even though it is more work.

Teaching financial literacy is Flo's passion, and she would say the extra work is well worth it. An added bonus for Flo is that she is well-supported. Flo's principal provides release time from teaching, and Flo only accepts pay from the county when she is working in the evening outside her regular teaching day and traveling to a variety of schools.

Flo also collaborates with the Maryland Council on Economic Education and with businesses, for whom financial literacy is so important. She is trying to develop community partners to help grow her work with both students and parents in poorer schools. "What I've learned in this work is that you never want anyone to be embarrassed or ashamed, you just need to listen to their stories and meet them where they are."

Flo is also a regular presenter at conferences and believes that attendance at conferences provides opportunities to see other teachers' passions. "What they are doing ignites your interests and passions."

"I don't know what I want to be doing five years from now," stated Flo matter-of-factly. But what she does know is that she wants to see financial literacy programs in schools across the state of Maryland. Flo expected her dream to be a reality and financial literacy to flourish across Baltimore County, then the state, in two years. "And while I don't know where I will be, I know I will be part of it! What I hope my own children are learning is that even in your 40s you can change your path. Life is full of opportunities. You just have to find your passion."

SUMMARY

As is true in teaching, we see in teacher leadership, too, that students and student learning are central to the important work that is undertaken by teacher leaders. Note that in the Framework *effective* teacher leaders *create, implement*, and *consistently advocate for* instruction that supports the needs of all learners. And while the content of the work changed in the four cases in this chapter, the teacher leaders' central focus on students and student learning was an element that remained constant across the work of all teacher leaders.

Teacher leaders are advocates. They advocate for changes in their schools and classrooms to meet the perceived needs of their students. However, in order to advocate and implement new ideas, or change, they must collaborate—not just with some of but with all the stakeholders in a community.

In fact, in many cases *effective* teacher leaders create a *collaborative culture*. To create a collaborative culture, teacher leaders must build trusting relationships. Sometimes building those relationships takes time. But many teacher leaders would argue it is worth it, because it is trust along with the credibility that is established over intentional work and time put in that provides a foundation for teachers to engage in collaboration and meaningful change with the teacher leader and with each other. And it is that meaningful change that brings about greater student learning and growth!

REFLECTIVE QUESTIONS AND APPLICATION

1. Reflect on the leadership of each teacher highlighted in this chapter. Place her on the rubric provided in the figures near the beginning of the chapter and justify your placement. Based on your placement,

what goal(s) might you set for each teacher leader to help her grow as a leader?

2. What observations did you make about each teacher leader in this chapter? What contributes to each leader's success? How could you utilize what you observed in your own setting?

3. Identify the vision and purpose of the work of each teacher leader. What aspects of each story resonated with you, and what did you learn from each story that might help in your own practice?

4. Self-assessment: reflecting on your own experiences and actions, place yourself on the rubrics provided in the figures near the beginning of this chapter. What area(s) of strength stand out, and what might you do to grow as a teacher leader in these areas?

REFERENCES

Boushey, G., & Moser, J. (2006) *The daily 5: Fostering literacy independence in the elementary grades*. Portsmouth, NH: Stenhouse Publishers.

Strike, K., Fitzsimmons, J., & Hornberger, R. (2019). *Identifying and growing internal leaders: A framework for effective teacher leadership*. Lanham, MD: Rowman & Littlefield.

Chapter Four

Teacher Leadership in Middle Level Education

This chapter presents four cases of middle school educators, but their cases represent different spheres of influence in their teacher leadership. Baochau Thomas shares her leadership journey of becoming the mathematics department chair and leading multi-grade-level curriculum development. Special educator Kelsey Baker explains her efforts to promote authentic learning for her students and her district's approach to developing teacher leadership through mentoring. Beth Heavin, a middle level English language arts teacher, describes her teacher leadership as a teacher union leader in helping teachers advocate for themselves. Finally, Kim Thomas, a middle level mathematics teacher who developed the Mathlicious approach, explains how she inspires learning in her students, colleagues, and the professional community.

Because of the diverse examples in this chapter's case studies, multiple domains and elements in the Framework for Effective Teacher Leadership (Strike, Fitzsimmons, & Hornberger, 2019) could readily apply. However, two interesting areas of intersection to examine are elements in "2b: Initiates and encourages growth in self and others" (see figure 4.1) and "4b: Demonstrates understanding of educational policy" (see figure 4.2).

In considering the leadership practices of these middle level educators, attend to the ways in which they view teacher leadership as extending outside their classrooms into different spheres of influence (i.e., school level, district level, community level, and policy level). Also evaluate how these middle level teachers have expanded their career pathways as they stepped into roles and responsibilities that might have been outside of many teachers' comfort zones. Self-evaluate the ways in which you might have approached these situations and the factors that appear to drive these types of leadership initiatives and risk taking.

2b. Initiates and encourages growth in self and others	Level of Performance			
Element	Ineffective	Initiating	Developing	Effective
Seeks appropriate leadership roles and opportunities extending beyond one's classroom	Fails to seek appropriate leadership roles and opportunities extending beyond one's classroom	Attempts but may not always seek appropriate leadership roles and opportunities extending beyond one's classroom	Models and upholds appropriate leadership roles and opportunities extending beyond one's classroom	Establishes and reinforces appropriate leadership roles and opportunities extending beyond one's classroom

Figure 4.1. Partial rubric for Framework for Effective Teacher Leadership (2b).

4b: Demonstrates understanding of educational policy	Level of Performance			
Element	Ineffective	Initiating	Developing	Effective
Builds bridges with administration and stakeholders to advance policies that influence quality instruction and student achievement	Fails to build bridges with administration and stakeholders to advance policies that influence quality instruction and student achievement	Attempts to build bridges with administration and stakeholders to advance policies that influence quality instruction and student achievement	Actively builds bridges with administration and stakeholders to advance policies that influence quality instruction and student achievement	Develops a collaborative culture that builds bridges with administration and stakeholders to advance policies that influence quality instruction and student achievement

Figure 4.2. Partial rubric for Framework for Effective Teacher Leadership (4b).

BAOCHAU THOMAS, MIDDLE SCHOOL MATHEMATICS TEACHER, CIMARRON MIDDLE SCHOOL, PARKER, COLORADO

Formal teacher leadership positions may be appointments teachers seek or appear unexpectedly. Baochau Thomas was finishing her first year as a seventh-grade mathematics teacher in a new middle school in a new state when she was selected as mathematics department chairperson and found herself facilitating the development and alignment of a standards-based curriculum. With 11 years of teaching experience, Baochau had never assumed a formal leadership role. She was experiencing a new teaching position for the first time in a decade and beginning to understand her students, the middle school, and Colorado's Academic Standards.

A National Board Certified Teacher, Baochau had earned her master's degree in teacher leadership and readily admits that she preferred not to lead initiatives but "to be the background person that quietly drives change behind the scenes." When she became the mathematics department chair at Cimarron Middle School in Parker, Colorado, and was tasked with formalizing the mathematics curriculum for 1,400+ students in grades 6, 7, and 8 in a department of 10 teachers, Baochau had mixed feelings:

> At first, I thought they were crazy. I'm new to the school, I'm new to this district, I'm new to this state. I thought 'no way' because I'm the type of person that if I'm going to do something, I'm going to do it right, I'm going to do it well, and I want to make it great for kids . . . I'm still learning the school and learning about the kids, and now I have to learn about the teachers. Because being a teacher leader is more than just your classroom, it's about the school. And I was very nervous.

Baochau highlighted three important contextual influences on her teacher leadership. First, as she explained, "Douglas County is site-based learning, every school does their own thing." Cimarron Middle School had an outdated math textbook with no formal curriculum.

Teachers were aligning their instruction to the Colorado Academic Standards but using personally chosen resources from programs piecemealed throughout the years. This made it difficult for families to understand the mathematics curriculum as their children moved across grade levels and teams. Formalizing and aligning a new school-wide curriculum was, as Baochau viewed it, a way to unify as a math department of four sixth-grade teachers, three seventh-grade teachers, and three eighth-grade teachers while also maintaining each teacher's autonomy.

A second unique aspect is that Douglas County Schools had adopted the use of the Emergenetics® profiles developed by Dr. Geil Browning and her colleagues (Browning, 2018). The program provides each teacher and administrator with a thinking and behavior profile based on questionnaire responses completed when the person is employed. These profiles are shared voluntarily so that educators better understand the ways they personally prefer to interact and approach decision making as well as know the different ways their colleagues lead their thinking and prefer to communicate and collaborate.

Each teacher's profile describes his/her relative degree in terms of four types of thinking: *analytical* (e.g., rational, learns by mental analysis), *structural* (e.g., practical, learns by doing), *conceptual* (e.g., intuitive, learns by experimenting), and *social* (e.g., relational, learns from others). Profiles also provide information on three continuums of interaction: *expressiveness* (quiet to gregarious), *assertiveness* (peacekeeping to driven), and *flexibility* (focused on welcoming change).

The third situational influence on this case study is that the department chair position is on a two-year rotation. Baochau clearly saw the development and implementation of a shared mathematics curriculum as her primary task during her term. She wanted to facilitate a smooth transition for the veteran teachers in the building in addition to laying the foundation for any future incoming teacher. Although she had met her colleagues within the last year, she knew that to be successful she needed to address the different needs and perspectives of each and every one of them.

For example, using her own Emergenetics® profile, Baochau understood that her analytical and structural strengths in thinking were useful, and she pulled from them:

> I think I know why I can do this because I lead with my structural and I lead with my analytical to bring about a brand new curriculum. To set it up and initiate it, you need someone who can structure it and think through it and see how it works. It ended up being an asset.

At the same time, Baochau knew that she had to flex into her social relational and conceptual thinking preferences in order to accomplish her goal as department chair. She solicited volunteers to begin the process of reviewing possible curriculum materials. Her analytical and structural approach told her: "I can't do this by myself. If I'm going to do this, I need a teacher at each grade level, we need a professional development day, and we need to look at all the grade level targets because everything still needs to be aligned with standards."

A team of four mathematics teachers (two sixth grade, Baochau representing seventh grade, and an eighth-grade teacher) formed the curriculum team.

This team looked at different types of curriculum materials, focusing on "how it would make our students better thinkers, better mathematicians" and began planning. Although the team benefited from the strong collaborative culture already established at Cimarron, Baochau still wanted input from all the teachers and found that some teachers readily expressed their concerns with the idea of new, formally adopted curriculum materials.

Understanding that some colleagues were naturally being focused, assertive, and expressive, Baochau assumed a stance that viewed using the new materials as a resource—not a change in teaching methods—and a way to help students get a common experience across teams. She readily acknowledged that one year was not sufficient to build strong interpersonal relationships, but because of the Emergenetics® profile information, she found that conflicts could be resolved and avoided.

As Baochau described one colleague who expressed her concern about the adoption of the same mathematics program, "She leads with structural and social—she teaches with group projects and hands-on learning. When we tried to put the curriculum map together, and she was upset because it wasn't how she teaches." But focusing on how the new materials could support her colleague's instruction addressed the frustration. Baochau explained that if she had not known that her colleague led her thinking in this way, it would have been easy to misconstrue intent.

At the end of her first year as mathematics department chair, the faculty decided to adopt the curriculum committee's recommended math program, for a couple of reasons. The teachers wanted the online and data analysis components that would help get feedback to the students more quickly, which would reduce grading time. Moreover, as Baochau explained, the driving factor in their decision was to help their students have more effective practice and develop resiliency, while meeting individual student needs. With the new curriculum identified, it became a repeating agenda item for discussion at department meetings and grade-level professional learning community (PLC) team meetings.

The summer between her first and second years as department chair, Baochau gave an extraordinary amount of time to planning for the new math program, assisting with curriculum guides, organizing the time line for trainings, and looking at what the teachers would need. Rather than view this as a burden, she saw it as something she needed to smoothly transition a department into the new school year. When considering her colleagues' needs, she anticipated their questions and concerns through the use of their Emergenetics® profiles.

At the same time, Baochau was not trying to create a finished product, but rather developing the necessary framework for the next school year. As she explained, "The individual PLC teams can take care of the fine tuning as they go along. I felt that it was my responsibility to make the start of the school year go as smooth as possible without dragging too many people away from their summer break."

Even with all the planning, consensus, and Baochau's extra summer work, her second year as chairperson, which was the first year of the new curriculum, was tumultuous. First there were issues with technology, such as problems with the math program's website and students logging on from home. Troubleshooting became so demanding for her that the department decided that Baochau needed help. By the end of the year, the department had met with the administrative team and decided that they needed someone to handle the technology. The principal agreed and created a stipend for mathematics department technology support.

There was also some parent resistance because the new math program was viewed as too difficult for their children. Additionally, the sixth-grade team became frustrated when they couldn't use the pacing guide because the sixth graders were not ready for the curriculum's first unit. As a result, the sixth-grade math PLC had to initiate a Unit 0 to support the students, supplementing the new curriculum. When the teachers expressed their concerns, Baochau interpreted it as an indication that she needed to do more to make this the best experience possible: "To get teachers to grow and to get teachers to be open-minded and try something new you've got to meet them where they are."

Baochau reassured the PLCs that the new materials were resources for building a common language. They wanted their students to understand why they needed to multiply by a reciprocal more than to follow a procedure to copy dot flop. Baochau checked in with PLCs frequently and asked questions, which varied by their needs. For teachers whose profiles told her they were more social-relational, Baochau geared questions more to "How are you doing," "How are you feeling," and "What did you think about this?"

For teachers who led with conceptual thinking, Baochau would ask, "How does this fit with what you've done in the past?" In other words, understanding where teachers were coming from and asking probing questions to get them what they needed was how Baochau viewed her leadership role. With one colleague who initially resisted and said, "I've never taught this [topic] before," Baochau knew her colleague led with analytical thinking, so she simply showed her the state standard, and her response was, "I don't know how I missed it."

Baochau also learned a lot from her colleagues. The department and grade level PLCs were meeting regularly and sharing their successes and failures with the new math curriculum. For example, the eighth-grade teachers found out from parents that some of the overachieving students would spend excessive amounts of time on practice problems to reach 100% accuracy when only

80% mastery was required. When the sixth- and seventh-grade teachers heard that feedback they adjusted their behavior.

Baochau decided not to assign the online homework and focused instead on using the formative and summative assessment online components. She found that her students received feedback more quickly and could use time making corrections as well as building resiliency and understanding, which were initial reasons for adopting the new program.

Communication, collaboration, and flexibility were key factors for celebration in the first year of implementation. Baochau believes that the successful communication and collaboration were already in place due to the strong collaborative culture in the building, but also partly due to everyone trained to use Emergenetics® and employing that language.

The teachers assumed there would always be colleagues who disagreed, but they put those debates in perspective by understanding each colleague's thinking as well as the department's thinking as a group. This shared knowledge made it easier to resolve disagreement and support change. Moreover, teachers were flexible and stated their opinions critically. Their feedback helped move the conversation forward and improve curriculum implementation, as Baochau explained:

> Sometimes you hear that the teachers who are asking questions are just causing trouble. But that's not how I thought. The teachers who are asking the questions are the ones who saw something I missed, and I value that a lot. Because I don't always ask, I'm flexible and will change, so having someone who is firm and focused and needs their question answered helped me understand their perspective and ask those questions myself.

Another way in which flexibility was instrumental to the successful implementation of the new curriculum was that there were no expectations about how teachers would use the new math program. This autonomy allowed teachers to use materials to their strengths. For example, one teacher was using the online videos to flip her classroom. For homework she assigned the videos, the students summarized them, then in class the next day they discussed the video and practiced the mathematics. In the end, teachers chose the components of the program that appealed to them and worked best in their classrooms.

Baochau was also flexible as department chairperson. She knew it would take hours outside of school to develop and implement the new math program, but not everyone needed to put in the same amount of time. Again, she focused on meeting the teachers' needs. Two sixth-grade teachers wanted to meet every Monday after school to problem solve the hurdles they were experiencing with the new materials. So Baochau met with them as needed.

She emphasized that it is important for different grade level PLCs to develop collaborations that work best for them and found that given this flexibility, everyone worked as a team within grade level and across the mathematics department. Baochau describes successful team thinking as, "Here's what our team is made up of. How do we honor each other's differences and make this the best year for kids?" Now the Cimarron Math Department is sought out by other departments that want to update their curricula.

At the end of her second and last year as chairperson, another teacher applied for the position. However, Baochau realized that she wanted to continue for another term. While she had been reluctant to assume a formal teacher leadership role, she wanted to continue:

> I just started something. I couldn't let it go, I wanted it to be fully developed. We started all this really cool stuff with our PLC work. . . . So I applied again. That took me by surprise because I didn't think I would. I was like, "OK, I only have two years to do this and then I'm out." But then I realized I can't let this go. So, they are giving me the opportunity to continue growing the math department and they gave the [technology] stipend to the other teacher who also applied. We are both veteran teachers and we make a good combo.

Finally, Baochau reconsidered the possibilities of teacher leadership. She never thought she would take a formal role like department chairperson, seeing herself as someone who helped in the background (e.g., being a mentor teacher, helping student teachers). Baochau thought she would be uncomfortable being the person formally driving change. However, after being department chair for two years, she looked ahead and said:

> It is really cool to be able to say, "this is where I see PLC work going." And "what can our collective brilliance do to make our school better?" We're going to really be in a good position—our math department is unified, we're speaking a common language, kids know exactly what to expect from 6th to 7th grade from 7th grade to 8th grade. I'm actually excited to be department chair next year.

KELSEY BAKER, MIDDLE SCHOOL SEVERE AND CROSS-CATEGORICAL SPECIAL EDUCATOR, EFFINGHAM UNIT 40 SCHOOL DISTRICT, EFFINGHAM, ILLINOIS

This case study demonstrates the results we can see in student learning if we have the courage to let go of what we know and explore what could be. Through a project known as The Coffee Cart, students in special education build communication skills, learn to make eye contact, talk to adults they wouldn't normally interact with, take and fill orders, make change, and keep inventory.

Effingham Unit 40 School District is a public district in rural, downstate Illinois. In a town of approximately 12,000 people, the middle school has about 675 students in grades 6–8. The school serves beyond the city limits and incorporates neighboring towns of 500–1,000 people within the county. The district enrolls 2,565 students, of whom 45% are low income, 19% are identified as having a disability, 2% are homeless, and 2% are English Language Learners. The racial/ethnic diversity is 92% white, 4% Hispanic, 2% two or more races, 1% black, and 1% Asian.

The district has a unique configuration of schools. There is an early learning center servicing PK–K, a grade school serving grades 1–2, another grade school that's PK–6, one middle school serving grades 6–8, and one high school serving grades 9–12.

Teacher leaders receive formal training within the Effingham Unit 40 School District. Training is determined based on a minimum of two years of experience and initiative shown with evolution of student learning through alternative measures. The teacher leaders are the trailblazers who step up and help other teachers. While there is no formal selection process or list of criteria, teacher leaders exhibit qualities such as engaging learners in exciting, fun ways in their classrooms.

The mentoring program for teacher leaders in Effingham Unit 40 School District is separate, specific, and more time-consuming. Mentoring trainings are longer in length. Formal teacher leader trainings were created by Chelle Beck, curriculum director, and Joe Fatheree, teacher of the year on staff, and cover three areas.

The first session overviews characteristics specific to teacher leaders. The first training is self-exploration focused on what it means to be a teacher leader. A DISC personality test uncovers the mystery of personality characteristics as well as how to interact with and address others who fall in the different areas of the DISC evaluation. This session helps the teacher leader evolve as a leader and better understand how to help others.

The second and third sessions further emphasize collaboration. The second session focuses on behavior a teacher leader exhibits, what characteristics he/ she possesses, and how to work better with others. The third session focuses on difficult conversations and how to help others when interactions between staff might be negative. Through this self-exploration, direct interactions can be viewed as sensitive or compassionate rather than gruff or abrasive.

Kelsey served as a middle school severe/cross-categorical special education (SPED) teacher. The school served grades 6–8, and Kelsey's caseload was comprised of students with autism, Down syndrome, learning disabilities, and traumatic brain injury. Kelsey grew concerned that her students were lacking content and knowledge to gain employment after completion of high school. In accordance with state law, students 14 years of age or older needed a transition plan for post–high school employment.

She began to research programs in the area and found that most were focused on serving students at the high school level. Programs she researched included a school store, coffee shop, and thrift store. Transitional opportunities at the middle school were not readily available; and as she researched further, she noted obstacles such as strict guidelines for handling food.

However, as Kelsey explored these options, she noted that the experience moved students from regurgitating information without learning it to applying it. Through daily practice came noted improvement. Kelsey observed a middle school and high school in neighboring Roxana, Illinois. She also collaborated with the three paraprofessionals in her classroom, who notedly kept her grounded throughout the planning process. When Kelsey began to dream beyond the available means, her paraprofessionals would reel her back in to focus on what was feasible. As a group, they focused on starting small.

In collaboration with her paraprofessionals, she identified the skills that needed improvement. The skills included eye contact, communication, talking and interacting with people they hadn't had contact with before, handling money (e.g., counting change), and time management (scheduling and availability). With this in mind, Kelsey opted to help her students start up a coffee cart. Through the coffee cart, skills were practiced in a hands-on way with practical experiences such as taking orders, filling orders, and using an iPad to keep up with inventory.

In planning for the coffee cart, Kelsey assisted her students in creating a survey. All staff were surveyed to see what items they would like to see offered, from coffee flavors to breakfast snacks of preference. A schedule was determined, and the coffee cart began. Within two days, students made $100 in revenue.

Time was an immediate factor. The coffee cart ran for 20–25 minutes in the early morning, while teachers had "check and connect time" and morning announcements were read. Since Kelsey's students were in SPED, they received their announcement information in a different way, so this was the opportune time to run their cart. However, the school posed the problem of being three floors, so at the conclusion of the announcements the class would return to their own classroom and be summoned with, "Hey, I wanted to order something and didn't see you." So a second cart was put in place. Kelsey's students added the delivery of the local paper to classrooms as a service.

When reflecting on the implementation of the project, Kelsey noted the importance of the teacher leader training. She understands that without that formal training, she might not have taken the initiative. Her head and heart both told her she had to say something, and that was the time to make the change. She explained that she had felt that way for six years, but only after the training did she feel it was time to go ahead and do it.

Collaborating with teachers in neighboring Roxana and the assistance and support of the three paraprofessionals were instrumental to the success of the coffee cart. Kelsey also noted that she hadn't received permission from any entity or person in the school or district. She saw something that needed to be done, and she moved on it.

The main area of focus chosen for Kelsey's students was communication. This area had been identified by the IEP process. Evidence was obtained through the use of the beginning of the year assessment, which was taken again later in the year, following the students' experience with the coffee cart. The rubric had a total of 12 points, with four areas assessed and each category worth 1, 2, or 3 points based on student behavior exhibited. For example, two of the areas included eye contact and responding back. All students showed gains on the rubric. Independence and communication were brought into the classroom through experience with the coffee cart.

Specific to student learning, staff noted improvement through three channels of evidence: communication skills, observation skills, and everyday life. The evidence was the gains on the assessment rubric used at the beginning and end of the year. In addition, students who were often overlooked or undervalued were now in the spotlight and feeling valued.

Colleagues were supportive and excited to see growth in the students. While the benefit to the students was evident and celebrated, the support did take a turn when the program received ongoing accolades through social media and local attention in the newspaper. Professional jealousy reared its ugly head when a colleague approached Kelsey and asked, "Who do you think you are?" Again, turning to her teacher leadership training, Kelsey was able to ask, "How can I help you create something within your program to experience the same success?"

The school and district were impacted in numerous ways: student attention, social media, newspaper and local press, community involvement, and even financial donations. People were contacting Kelsey and asking if they could donate to her program because they were so impressed with the benefits to the student population she served. In addition, the state of Illinois hosted a Powered By Teach to Lead Summit in April 2018, and Kelsey's class was not only highlighted at the summit but ran their coffee cart during the keynote speech.

Kelsey has recognized the power of teacher leadership. When we utilize with each other the strengths between us, we improve our district. The motto of the district is Together Everyone Achieves More (TEAM). The formal teacher leader training Kelsey received provided the skills and confidence for difficult conversations. She learned how to build and foster relationships with coworkers and staff and to identify ways to build on what they were doing. She was able to help others implement ideas within their own programs.

Building new curricular programs emerged as a simple fix to a complex problem: students weren't learning the skills through the old strategies, and Kelsey noted that it's okay not to teach prescribed curriculum every minute of the day. Instead, it's more important to build innovative, creative programs that embrace different instructional approaches to meet the needs of different types of people.

Teacher leader training provided the insight to approach different types of people, not to diagnose them, but to work with them in ways that fit their needs and help them grow. Furthermore, the training helped Kelsey with building the confidence to reach out and explore additional employment opportunities.

Kelsey moved into a principal position for the SPED cooperative to which she was once a contributing member and is trying to build relationships with staff. As an evaluator, Kelsey is working to establish relationships, build on their teaching, and then evaluate their teaching. Kelsey understands the need to help move people out of their comfort zone; think outside the box; and coach them so student learning is maximized, they experience success, and they discover how to be the best educators they can be.

Looking at a five-year plan, Kelsey is anxious to implement a teacher leadership training program into her new school, specific to SPED. In a smaller school, training can create big change. The training will create a team of teacher leaders who could help build the program, spotlight strengths of faculty and staff, and move teachers from the familiarity of their program to outside their comfort zone by highlighting natural leadership of self and others.

BETH HEAVIN, LANGUAGE ARTS TEACHER AND TEACHER ASSOCIATION COPRESIDENT, CENTER GROVE COMMUNITY SCHOOL CORPORATION, GREENWOOD, INDIANA

For this case study, middle school language arts teacher Beth Heavin shared her experiences as a teacher association leader in helping teachers advocate for themselves and, in the case of association building representatives, for their colleagues. This case study highlights how each teacher's situation is unique, with teachers finding themselves faced with complex issues in different school contexts. What Beth works toward in promoting self-advocacy among K–12 teachers highlights how advocacy can be seen as professional self-empowerment and how advocacy benefits both teachers and students.

Beth has been a middle school teacher for 15 years and active in the teacher association (Indiana State Teachers Association) in her district and on the state level for as many as 20 years. Since 2016, she has been copresident of her district's teachers' association. Prior to that time, she served as the association's vice president and legislative liaison for 12 years. In her first year as copresident Beth co-served with an elementary teacher (Terry), and since 2017 she has co-served with another elementary teacher (Peggy).

Center Grove Community School Corporation is located in Greenwood, Indiana, southwest of Indianapolis. As a K–12 school district with one high school, two middle schools, and five elementary buildings with a sixth under construction, it is a relatively large (more than 8,500 students) and growing district. The student population is primarily Caucasian (84.9%) and middle class (20.2% free/reduced lunch).

As the copresident of the 200+ teachers in the local teachers' association, Beth's experiences in helping teachers advocate for themselves have been in two general ways: advocating for themselves in teacher-principal evaluation meetings and advocating as building faculty faced with demands that consume resources and negatively affect their teaching.

Advocacy in all cases can be about minor issues or have major consequences. For example, Beth explained that in a teaching evaluation conference, advocacy can be as simple as responding to an offhand comment by the evaluator. Or it may require more initiative and a prepared response, such as when the teacher is evaluated as needing improvement and doesn't believe the evidence indicates a low rating.

Beth gave the example of a simple way to advocate during an evaluation meeting being to point out the specific wording on the rubric. For example, an indicator (the district uses a modified version of the Danielson Framework) states the daily learning objectives have to be posted, and this can be done in the plan book or on the board. However, a teacher may get a lower evaluation in that category because the evaluator didn't like the way objectives were posted (i.e., prefers one place over another), or the evaluator wants specific wording (e.g., today we will . . ., or we know we have it when . . .).

So self-advocacy can be as simple as pointing out that the rubric needs to be followed, and these preferences are not part of the rubric. But without self-advocacy, Beth is often called in because a "needs improvement" rating needs to be addressed. What might have been a brief, assertive response becomes a teacher's annual evaluation rating that needs formal discussion and outside advocacy.

Advocacy, however, is not always about something as personal as an evaluation; it can be about building, even district-wide initiatives. And Beth has observed multiple times that entire building faculties may not advocate for themselves as a collective. For example, Beth described one instance where administration decided to push in 45 additional minutes of a writing program.

She worked to support the teachers by asking questions about where the time for planning and assessment would be found for this additional instruction. At first the questions weren't addressed, but eventually the decision was made that instructional aides would be utilized for some recess times so that a couple days each week the elementary teachers would not have recess duty and they could plan for the writing program.

However, every year since the recess release time was agreed upon, teachers across the elementary buildings have had to continue to advocate for themselves. Some principals will start off a school year scheduling the aides without considering the time for the teachers' recess breaks. And the teachers would not remind them of the agreement and advocate for their agreed upon planning time.

Even three years after the recess release time was agreed upon, two elementary buildings were still experiencing this reoccurring problem, which seemed to appear where there was an advocacy vacuum. One of the barriers to advocacy in these situations Beth found is that once the aides have been assigned, the teachers do not want to advocate for their recess release because they feel they are removing the aides from students.

A barrier that Beth often sees in teachers' reluctance to self-advocate is a subservient mind-set. Teachers focus on putting others' needs first, especially their students', forgetting that their own needs are just as important for student success. Part of a subservient mind-set also seems to be an unwillingness to have people upset or to appear to be a burden.

As Beth explains to teachers, "You have to take care of yourself. . . . If you don't stand up and say I have to have that time, then what will happen is more will be piled on." And as more is expected of teachers, their ability to effectively teach and support their students will dwindle. At some point teachers will have to say no, and Beth believes that part of her leadership is helping them recognize that "no" needs to be said earlier rather than later.

Another core part of supporting teacher advocacy, as Beth explained, is helping teachers suspend worrying about what others will think about their position. Where she has seen teachers successfully advocate for their building as well as self-advocate for themselves has been when their perspectives seemed to shift to caring more about the impact of their argument and less about what others thought of them making the argument.

Beth described a recent instance of a relatively new elementary building association representative who had become a strong voice for her colleagues.

She saw this teacher as helping to make a radical shift in culture. Although Beth does not take personal credit when teachers successfully step into advocacy, she and Peggy, the other association copresident, have worked together to make sure all the building representatives have the tools and support they need to advocate.

Prior to the start of each school year, Beth and Peggy have scheduled a meeting for building representatives. The primary message that Beth wants to get across is, "You have to stand up for yourselves. You have to try it first. Of course, I'll always be there. Of course, I'll come in, but you have to try to rein it in on your own."

Beth believes that many teachers, and especially elementary teachers, hesitate in their own self-advocacy because they believe their principal's or assistant principal's first reaction will be not to budge. They will face resistance. However, Beth's experience has been that if a teacher's reaction can be firm and show evidence, most administrators will listen and change their minds. In many ways, opportunities for self-advocacy are linked to school norms and culture. At the same time, Beth acknowledges that there are individual differences in teachers' willingness to argue a point and deal with conflict.

When asked how she approaches helping individual teachers build advocacy skills and attitudes, Beth responded, "We talk a lot." Beth said that she and Peggy know the teachers are coming to them with valid concerns. They always start by explaining to teachers that advocacy begins by pointing out what has already been decided in school documents or school corporation minutes. Nonetheless, teachers often second-guess themselves. If the principal resists their point or evidence, even mildly (e.g., "I don't think we have to do that"), then some teachers withdraw and will ask Peggy or Beth to sit in on their meetings to discuss these issues.

The constant support for self-advocacy is why Beth and Peggy work so hard to help building representatives advocate within their buildings and support their colleagues in self-advocacy.

For example, when an administrator decided to introduce a new mathematics workshop in addition to the adopted curriculum, they modeled advocacy by asking questions of the teachers: How many stations are you going to need to plan? When the teachers answered 10 stations each week, they followed up by asking: When will you plan for the 10 stations? Where will you get all the materials needed? The building representative had to help the teachers see that this was not a tenable request and that the teachers needed to work out the details and potential conflicts proactively rather than respond to them negatively.

Another important part of supporting teachers' advocacy is supporting their confidence. Beth explained that when the building representatives are brought together, she tells them, "You're a hero. Your colleagues are looking to you and counting on you to know what you are doing. You're the first line because you know what you are talking about and you know what your principal's decisions are going to do in your building."

She also emphasizes how every building is going to be unique. Their problems will be different because although the curriculum and expectations are the same, there is a lot of flexibility in how to achieve outcomes.

As Beth entered her third year as copresident she saw the results of focusing on helping teachers advocate for themselves and their schools. She believes these positive outcomes are due to a change of mind-set. That change is one in which advocacy is seen as something teachers do for themselves, not something they ask others to do for them.

Finally, Beth emphasized that an essential tool for advocacy is information. She described how several years ago as copresident of the association she found that she was always trying to catch up and learn what was going on. Now she and Peggy focus on keeping teachers informed, so they know what is coming and they know what decisions have been made as far as curriculum and processes.

Beth explained her own transformation: "[N]ow I feel like I am *with* the administrators. Even though it means a lot more work. I understand what's happening and I've got the teachers with me. I'm not talking about agreeing or disagreeing with the administration, but I understand them. And when that happens teachers know that I am telling them as much as I know, then they feel more confident."

Two additional key components of advocacy that Beth emphasized are documenting and listening. Beth noted that teachers are very trusting, but miscommunication is common, so they need good documentation and to learn to listen first.

Beth has seen just how critical documentation is in advocacy. Saving the communications in which new initiatives are announced and outlined is important (e.g., saving the email that says, "We're going to . . ."). Beth explained that she sends e-mails to administrators to help document a shared understanding and keep a time line. She views this type of documentation as being proactive and reaching out to the principals and assistant principals to clarify what they meant and avoid miscommunication (e.g., responding with an e-mail that asks, "Can you give me some clarification?").

When asked how she would bullet point the key components for teacher advocacy, Beth responded:

- *Be your first line of offense.* If you feel something is not right, then chances are it isn't, and that needs to be addressed. Try to fix it on your own.

- *Always be collaborative.* Present your best possible self. Don't believe that everyone is looking out for you. And don't believe that everyone is out to get you. Ask others to help you listen better. Try out your ideas first. It is good to have someone you trust with you in a difficult situation.
- *Communication is key.* Talk to your evaluator or administrator when you sense a problem might be arising. Always be positive. Know what you will say and how you will say it.
- *Do your homework.* Check your facts. Then double-check the facts. Write out what you will say.

As Beth explains to the teachers she supports, "I'm not going in to intercede for you. I'm going in to be your ears. I might tell you that I didn't hear it the same way as you." She wants them to be prepared to stand up for themselves because there are a lot of forces at play and they are the ones responsible for their own careers. In her own words, "I see these capable, compassionate, brilliant educators and say, stand up for yourself. Stand up for yourself. Advocacy gives you a feeling of empowerment. And then you'll be better in your own classroom."

KIM THOMAS, MIDDLE LEVEL
MATH TEACHER, PEORIA, ILLINOIS

Kim Thomas teaches math to 60 sixth- through eighth-grade students at an alternative school in central Illinois boasting one of the poorest zip codes across the state. Her students have all been expelled or administratively placed in her classroom. Kim's message to all is that "teachers plus students equal dreams coming true." She reports, "I never was a cheerleader in middle or high school but look at me now—I am a *TEACHEER!*" Kim believes that *every child deserves a pep rally.* For most of her students, there have been many no's and don'ts, and they come into her classroom expecting the same. Boy are they in for a surprise!

Kim's district is the fourteenth largest district in the state, with a population of 13,222 students, 69% of whom are from low income families. Kim has spent her entire teaching career in this district. Her passion for this community began on her first day of student teaching, when she arrived at her school and her cooperating teacher was absent. Kim recalls, "I talked to the substitute, picked up the lesson plans, and began to teach. It was the worst day ever!"

A student called her a *#!!# and she taught on. Kim says, "I cried later— no one had ever said anything like that to me before." The student was suspended, and when he returned to school, he apologized and Kim replied, "What? Why I've forgotten all about it." So taken aback by Kim's positive attitude and winning smile was that student that he became one of her best. That was the beginning of what would come to be known as "Mathlicious-ness": the idea that learning has to be positive and fun if you want kids to learn math—really love math and learn it.

Kim started as an elementary teacher, but after two years when an opening occurred in the seventh and eighth grade, Kim was drawn to teach in that class and went back to school to pick up her middle school and math endorsements. But once again, on the first day of class, the students walked into her math class saying things like, "Arghhhhh-math! Math *sucks!*" Kim didn't know then, but math would be the hill on which she would stand for some 2 x 10 years.

And everything that could be *mathified* would be. "When kids enter my classroom, I tell them to just give me 1/60 of an hour to rotate their negative parabolas into positive ones." She continues, "One positive > than any negative—it's mathematical so it has to be true." Kim explains that teachers are the 3-D superheroes for all kids. "You know, length x width x height. Teachers go to any length for kids, their arms are always open wide, and every day they reach new heights."

Kim immerses her students in math and lets them know she cares. "Be the best fraction of a kid's day" is Kim's mantra. For Kim that means not only remembering something positive about each kid every day, but for her students, school will be one of the best parts of their day.

Kim is never content to be done with her lesson plans until she finds a creative edge for each and every lesson she teaches. For example, Mathentine's Day is a celemathbration of a 3-D Valentine. On the net of their 3-D heart, she instructs students to write their favorites on a variety of topics. Then she has them cut out the net of the cube and fold it. To complete the heart, they figure out what size circle and rectangle is needed to create the cylinder.

Kim's students discover the diameter of the circle must be equal to the side of each square face on the cube. They also discover the circumference of the circle must be congruent to the length of the rectangle, and the width of the rectangle must be equal to the edge of the cube. Kim exclaims, "I get exponential mathbumps as my students learn abstract math concepts and get excited while engaging in a hands-on math learning process."

Kim continues, "I'm really trying to get our district to be more engaged in teacher-led rather than administrative-led initiatives." Kim shares that what really helped her develop her leadership beyond the master's degree in teacher leadership that she earned was her first principal:

He came into my room and said, "Kim, you have to share what you are doing with others." I just assumed that everyone was doing what I did. But he said, "No—they're not." He encouraged me to share my ideas and strategies with others. With his prodding I began sharing strategies on Institute Days—not to make me look a certain way but because of kids. Kids deserve to be taught in a way that helps them learn best. Teachers would also come to my classroom and observe me, and I'd share everything.

Another passion for Kim is advocating for alternative programs and the kids who fill those classrooms. Kim describes her students in this mathematical way: "My classroom is filled with diverse angles, some acute and some obtuse. Regardless of the angle, it's my job to take them from where they are to where they need to be. Understanding each diverse angle and using my Mathlicious approach lets kids know that I see their future potential and don't dwell on their past mistakes."

Kim believes that you have to address social and emotional learning before you can address academics. "My kids come to school having had many traumatic events already, so I have to give them more positives." Kim walks the talk, or as she would say, she runs the rhombus with kids. "At the first angle you are assisting with behavior growth (replacing anger, cussing, fighting, . . . whatever negative behaviors they come with). Then at the next angle you are meeting social emotional learning needs, rounding the next angle you address academic growth and then you slide into home plate—and feel the joy of success!"

Kim serves as a coach, mentor, and motivational speaker. She has been recognized as teacher of the year and is a published author. When asked about her five-year plan, Kim responded, "I'll be right here in my classroom, but I'll be better because that's what I strive to do every day just like my students!" And, of course, there would be a second book.

SUMMARY

The middle school case studies in this chapter illustrate an array of teacher leadership, from classroom-based approaches and departmental curricular reform to implementing school-wide instructional practices and district-wide teacher advocacy. One important way in which these cases are interconnected is that each teacher leader supported professional growth in his/her colleagues and peers, as defined in the Framework for Effective Teacher Leadership (Strike, Fitzsimmons, & Hornberger, 2019). The ability to motivate and lead a group of professionals to try new ideas, take risks, and make change happen is fundamental to teacher leadership.

The case studies in this chapter extend Fairman and Mackenzie's (2012) findings that regardless of context, teacher leaders primarily engage in leadership in two important ways: by improving student outcomes and enhancing teacher professional development. While some teacher leaders may promote growth in more formal roles, such as Baochau as department chair and Beth as teacher association copresident, other teachers promote changes through connecting their students' needs to the greater school community, like Kelsey did with her students' coffee cart and Kim did with Mathlicious.

Across their various spheres of influence, these teacher leaders highlighted the multiple contexts of leadership that are organized in *The Teacher Leadership Competencies* (Center for Teaching Quality, National Board for Professional Teaching Standards, & National Education Association, 2014): instructional leadership, policy leadership, and association leadership.

These middle school case studies also illustrated how each teacher leader's professional growth, specifically in leadership, can be developed and supported. Again, like the case study analysis in Fairman and Mackenzie (2012), this chapter's cases show how teacher leaders' own learning is extended "beyond content and pedagogy" (p. 243) through their leadership.

Moreover, the teacher leaders in this chapter highlighted how their own preparation in leadership through professional development and advance study became translated to their providing or utilizing professional development opportunities to support the growth of their colleagues. In sum, each teacher's leadership journey involved the support of others and finding ways to leverage her knowledge and inspire others to make a difference.

REFLECTIVE QUESTIONS AND APPLICATION

1. Reflect on the leadership of each teacher highlighted in this chapter. Place the teachers on the rubrics provided in the figures near the beginning of the chapter and justify your placement.
2. Self-assessment: reflecting on your own experiences and actions, place yourself on the rubrics provided in the figures near the beginning of this chapter. What area(s) of strength stand out, and what might you do to improve or obtain additional experience?
3. Identify the vision and purpose of the work of each teacher leader.
4. What were some of the challenges in translating each teacher leader's vision into operational terms? What alternatives or changes might you recommend? Is this something you have, or something that could work in your own setting? If not, what changes would need to be made for it to work in your own setting?

5. What contributes to each leader's success?
6. What aspects of each story resonated with you, and what did you learn from each story that might help in your own practice?
7. What observations have you made in looking at the leadership highlighted in this chapter, specific to teacher leadership at the middle school level, compared to that shared in other chapters? Would you say teacher leadership is easier to plan and implement within the middle school setting? Why or why not?

REFERENCES

Browning, G. (2018). *Work that works: Emergineering a positive organizational culture*. Hoboken, NJ: John Wiley & Sons.

Center for Teaching Quality, National Board for Professional Teaching Standards, & National Education Association. (2014). *The teacher leadership competencies* [PDF file]. Retrieved from http://www.nea.org/home/61346.htm

Fairman, J. C., & Mackenzie, S. V. (2012). Spheres of teacher leadership action for learning. *Professional Development in Education, 38*(2), 229–46.

Strike, K., Fitzsimmons, J., & Hornberger, R. (2019). *Identifying and growing internal leaders: A framework for effective teacher leadership*. Lanham, MD: Rowman & Littlefield.

Chapter Five

Teacher Leadership at the High School Level

This chapter focuses on teacher leadership within the high school setting. In the case studies provided in this chapter you will read about Mary Abbott-Wagner, who created a teacher education program where students earn college credit and experience field work while still attending high school. You will also read about Daniele Massey, who focused her project on increasing student engagement in the virtual setting, and Ronald Towns, whose leadership in mathematics supports a department culture where teachers share data and use the inquiry cycle to improve student learning. Finally, we share Lilly's story of how teacher leadership has impacted the ability to mentor new and novice teachers.

The case studies in this chapter are examples of Domain 2, Professional Growth of Self and Others in *Identifying and Growing Internal Leaders: A Framework for Effective Teacher Leadership* (Strike, Fitzsimmons, & Hornberger, 2019). As you read each of the case studies, consider "2a: Demonstrates leadership" (see figure 5.1) and "2c: Engages and supports the development of future leaders" (see figure 5.2).

Reflect on the leadership of each teacher highlighted in this chapter. Place the case studies on the rubric in the figures and justify your placement. Examine the impact of the teacher leader's decisions and the opportunities afforded in his/her context. Consider successes and alternatives or changes you might recommend as an observer. Also consider possibilities for your own setting.

2a: Demonstrates Leadership	Level of Performance			
Element	Ineffective	Initiating	Developing	Effective
Supports innovative thinking and risk-taking efforts	Does not support innovative thinking and risk-taking efforts	Limited support of innovative thinking and risk-taking efforts	Actively encourages support of innovative thinking and risk-taking efforts	Builds a culture supportive of innovative thinking and risk-taking efforts

Figure 5.1. Partial rubric for Framework for Effective Teacher Leadership (2a).
Copyright © Strike, Fitzsimmons, & Hornberger, 2019.

2c. Engages and supports the development of future leaders	Level of Performance			
Element	Ineffective	Initiating	Developing	Effective
Demonstrates interpersonal effectiveness through articulation of ways to support others to build competence, confidence and capacity	Fails to demonstrate interpersonal effectiveness through articulation of ways to support others to build competence, confidence and capacity	Inconsistently demonstrates interpersonal effectiveness through articulation of ways to support others to build competence, confidence and capacity	Shows evidence of interpersonal effectiveness through articulation of ways to support others to build competence, confidence and capacity	Advances leadership capacity and interpersonal effectiveness through articulation of ways to support others to build competence, confidence and capacity

Figure 5.2. Partial rubric for Framework for Effective Teacher Leadership (2c).
Copyright © Strike, Fitzsimmons, & Hornberger, 2019.

MARY ABBOTT-WAGNER, TEACHER EDUCATION PROGRAM LEADER, NORTHWEST CAREER AND TECHNICAL ACADEMY, CLARK COUNTY, LAS VEGAS, NEVADA

This case study is focused on a teacher preparation program implemented at a high school in Las Vegas. Through development of this program, Mary focused on being part of the solution rather than complaining about the problem (teacher recruitment and retention). Mary's mantra, shared with her students who will one day be educators themselves, is "Be passionate. Work with intent."

Northwest Career and Technical Academy (NWCTA) started more than 11 years ago as a magnet school. Since the time of its opening, six additional magnet schools have opened. The school serves high school grade levels (9–12) and is located in urban Las Vegas, Nevada. NWCTA functions on student interest and buy-in from the staff and students.

The demographics of the school reflect that the student population is approximately 36% Hispanic, 32% white, 13% Asian, 9% black, and 8% two or more races (2% not reporting on the 2017–2018 Accountability Report Card). Free and reduced lunch is used by 35.6% of the student population. Staff are encouraged to get to know the students personally and build relationships in a way that is different from most schools. Northwest Career and Technical Academy prides itself on creating a safe, family environment.

At Northwest Career and Technical Academy, every program has a program leader who serves as an expert. There are no requirements to serve as the department head, as many of the teachers on staff come from the industry and are there to teach the students their trade. For example, the culinary teacher would have worked in business, had restaurant experience, and then gone back for teacher licensure.

There is an understanding among the staff that lecture is not the best methodology to teach the students at Northwest Career and Technical Academy. At NWCTA it's not about content but about building relationships. Personality is instrumental and cannot be taught. Content can be known well but not effectively shared with the students.

Teacher leaders serving at Northwest Career and Technical Academy must be lifelong learners willing to continue to actively participate in professional learning. They must be flexible, supportive, and serve as mentors to the young, aspiring students. Among other things, teacher leaders are there to support other teachers, provide staff development, and mentor the new or struggling teachers.

Mary was foundational in the opening of Northwest Career and Technical Academy. On the first day of school, without even having taught a class yet, Mary asked her principal if he would be putting a teacher education program together. She expressed that she really wanted to do it and thought she was ready. The reply from her principal was if she wanted to do it, it was her baby.

Mary pulled all of the course syllabi for teacher education programs at another magnet school (Clark High School) and was given the freedom to decide what the program would look like at Northwest Career and Technical Academy. The standards were reviewed, and from there the materials were decided upon. Mary e-mailed professors to gain perspective on course materials and possible textbooks and utilized their input to design college-level courses.

The first year was dedicated to working on planning the program. The program originally started serving grades 9 and 10 but transitioned to serve freshman-seniors. While not all students were served at once, Mary had to prepare for them. When the program began, teachers gladly assisted.

A few years after the program began, a full-day kindergarten was implemented within the high school setting. A full-time kindergarten teacher was hired to teach the kindergarten students, and also to oversee the lesson plan writing and implementation from the high school juniors and seniors. Mary, having a background in English, had her students focus on lesson plans for the kindergarten literacy centers, which included reading, writing, word work, poetry, and art/math. Students created lessons and then had the opportunity to discuss those lessons with Mary, make changes, prepare all materials, and then teach their lessons to the kindergarten students. The students could see what worked and what didn't, and conversations could surround their experience. In addition, the Special Education Department chair allowed the teacher education students to work with her POST students (special needs program for students ages 18–22). The students mentored the special needs students throughout their junior and senior years as well.

All of this led to a local partnership sought out by the University of Nevada–Las Vegas (UNLV), which was interested in Mary's students who were learning all of these skills before high school graduation. Mary wanted to build a program to home-grow students who wanted to be teachers to fill the gap created by the local teacher shortage. UNLV had the same determination to keep Las Vegas's best and brightest students who had already expressed a desire to become teachers.

Mary not only taught the curriculum needed in the high school teacher education program, but also taught the following coursework for UNLV (during the students' school day) so the students could begin work on a bachelor's degree before ever leaving the high school setting: EDU 201, Introduction to Elementary Education; EDU 203, Introduction to Special Education; EDU 280, Valuing Cultural Diversity; and EDU 210, Nevada School Law. When the teacher education students graduated from NWCTA, they had two years of kindergarten practicum, two years of special education practicum, and 11 college credits.

The program started small, but over the course of 10 years, it became a desired program at NWCTA, and one that fills up quickly. In fact, in the 2018–2019 school year, the program has expanded to twice its size (60 new freshmen per year instead of 30). In working with the local university, students now earn college credit within their high school English, history, and science classes.

No data are available to show the number of students who actually entered the field of education. Reports provided within the project are specific to professional development and technology. However, students do keep in touch with Mary, and they often have entered related fields such as psychology or social work, if not the field of education.

One ongoing challenge in the creation of the program was funding. There was never enough funding for what was really needed. The teacher education program became a strand under Career and Technical Education (CTE) and now receives federal monies through Perkins under the Education and Training strand. The curriculum for Teach 1 was implemented in the 2017–2018 school year with the freshman class. Teach 2 and Teach 3 were to be added in the following school years. The program is recognized not only for the college credit earned, but also for the CTE distinction upon completion of the program.

Another challenge was to locate materials that represented the best of the best. Finding texts, activities, etc., that were timely and relevant to the classroom took extensive research. A third challenge revolved around acceptance and support from others: colleagues (local), state administrative positions within the Department of Education, and the state CTE department.

While acceptance and support were a challenge, the level of support the program received from the (founding) principal, the Special Education Department, faculty as a whole, the local kindergarten teacher who scheduled and provided a forum for practicums, and the school itself was both evident and a huge benefit to the implementation.

The impact of the program spanned from student learning and teacher preparation to colleagues and the district itself. The program provided the basis for a career, and the staff, students, school, and district worked together to make it happen.

Intended outcomes were twofold: learn it, love it so (a) you can go to school and (b) skills learned can apply to other areas and contexts. For some students within the program, it helps them determine what they don't want to do. This is not a bad thing, as the students have experiences throughout the program that help them to determine if teaching is really their passion. It is much better to find that out during high school than during the last year of college, when it's late to make a change.

As Mary stated, there is so much to share! Teacher leaders must be flexible, reflective, kind, and responsible. Through service as a teacher leader, one becomes a better teacher. If you find that someone doesn't know something, teach them. If they don't get it, train them. Help them understand the experience they're having and ensure them they're not bothering you.

Mary shared the importance of being truthful, especially if you don't know something. Technology is important but won't help with classroom management. Be innovative and encourage problem-based learning. Keep current with what's going on in your field and move *with* the kids you teach.

Mary has received nominations for awards, such as the Heart of Education Award. Nominated by her students, she was touched but clear that she didn't do what she did for an award. Winning awards wasn't the goal. Having served as a mentor was what was important. Mary stressed that teaching is a gift. Experiences vary for each one of us, but we need to move people out of their comfort zone and be a catalyst for change.

DANIELE MASSEY, MATHEMATICS TEACHER, VIRTUAL HIGH SCHOOL, PRINCE WILLIAM COUNTY, QUANTICO, VIRGINIA

This case study focuses on the need for increased student engagement in online learning. The teacher leader was driven by questions focused on how we measure student engagement in online learning, how we motivate teachers to engage students in online learning, and how we know students get what we want them to get.

Daniele teaches mathematics in an online setting for a worldwide, federally funded school system. Face-to-face learning is supported in the system as well. The school system is suburban, private, and unique in that it does have tuition-paying members, but not all students pay tuition. The school focuses on a specific population, serving those who have connections with actively serving military personnel or critical civilian support positions. The geographic areas with such personnel are Quantico, Virginia; Sembach, Germany; and Okinawa, Japan. Though identified as a high school, the school serves grades 7–12. Students are from around the world, and are 4% Hispanic, 4% African American, and 92% Caucasian. The student population is under 50 students and has remained flat. However, due to the number of military bases closed in recent years, the number of courses offered online has nearly doubled in that same time frame, growing to 76 courses now offered. Students use online courses for permanent change of station (PCS) or transition, regular enrollment, and course recovery.

Recently the school system created formal teacher leader roles to support mathematics and literacy curriculum. There has been a tiered approach to the Common Core State Standards, which the school system calls College and Career Readiness Standards. At the middle and high school levels as well as at the elementary level, mathematics and literacy are a focus. Teacher leader roles have been created to help support department chairs, grade level chairs, and community school improvement chairs. Teacher leadership is not necessarily informal, but leaders haven't had formal teacher leader titles given to them. The term *teacher leader* is new to the organization over the last few years.

Daniele serves as a mathematics teacher for Algebra I, Financial Algebra, and Algebra I Recovery. Named State Teacher of the Year in 2013, Daniele uses this platform to work with other teachers of the year to develop teacher leadership and recognize great teaching throughout the organization. She serves as one of the organizers for an annual Teacher Leader Summit and serves on School Improvement Committee no. 2, which focuses on increasing student engagement in online learning.

An accreditation visit drove the initial conversation. The visit identified that student learning styles weren't being met. The school was charged to look at student learning styles and then adjust courses or adopt courses at more engaging levels.

A formalized action plan was created. First the teachers aligned with the calendar in order to meet quarterly. There was a variety of teachers involved, including online classroom teachers, an instructional designer, an assistant principal, and a special education support teacher. The first year was slow moving as the teachers worked to identify what engagement even means.

Due to the nature of the school, student survey was not an available tool. However, assessments were readily available. The committee searched for what type of data were already available and what data could be collected. Once the data were reviewed, the questions turned to what the teachers were saying and what the students were saying. The committee recognized that the accreditation report was one report and a great start to the conversation, but it did not define them or their work. Their goal was to further their understanding of what the data provide and what students actually want and need.

In 2010, as an accredited school fully administering degrees, the norm was to purchase courses from vendors. Vendor courses were found to be very limited and not easily adjusted, so teacher leaders took on this charge. Through a creative approach, teachers worked together to move away from rigid, canned programs that did not meet students' learning styles and were flat, in that all students did was read, to encouraging and requiring student engagement. A large factor was the understanding of the importance of building in teacher presence.

Over a two-year period, teachers have focused on building relationships and showing the personality of the instructor, to build teacher presence in ways such as welcome videos. Self-exploration of free programs such as Screencast-o-matic, Camtasia, and Audacity has provided the necessary tools. Teachers are encouraged—and expected—to share their sense of humor, have fun, and be themselves.

In order to work together, teachers had to first define student engagement, then provide examples. A third need was to create a teacher tool box based on four areas: assessment, first and last days of school, classroom management, and instruction. Collaborative ways to connect were put in place, but it took some time for teachers to build their own relationships to be comfortable with—and vulnerable in—sharing ideas. As a teacher leader, this was a way Daniele stood out, as she put herself out there first. This not only modeled for others, but also provided a safe environment for one and all to share ideas.

Other ways Daniele provided leadership were providing a weekly staff newsletter and encouraging colleagues to share articles, sharing information such as infographics, asking questions, and networking with other teacher leaders.

Challenges faced by Daniele included keeping the committee interested. Project management called for the committee to communicate what they were doing. This particular project didn't have tangible boxes to tick off but instead relied on a network of professionals working together. Through a variety of personal learning networks that included social media and professional networks such as Teacher of the Year, the committee explored what student engagement looks like in other schools and shared relevant literature. An orientation for new teachers was created for expectations to be shared and results to be more immediate.

Evidence that the teachers were making progress toward the outcomes included use of local assessment data. A school goal specific to the increase of literacy and writing through a 6+1 Writing Traits rubric both provided meaningful feedback and monitored progress. Use of beginning- and end-of-year prompts provided the opportunity to score the writing. Keywords were pulled to analyze, and teachers were asked for feedback on their experiences.

Other evidence included the amount of time students were logged into their course, how many minutes the student invested while taking a quiz or test, and student perceptions, such as when they expressed frustration. The philosophy of seat time versus engagement was a focus for professional discussions, as was the idea of mirroring versus balancing engagement.

From the accreditation report there were three main areas identified as areas of improvement. The first was to demonstrate to the accreditation team that will come back in 2020 that there has been progress from flat coursework to engagement of the learner. Within this area is a demonstration that the online learning is meeting the learning styles of the learners.

A second area of focus is to address professional discourse. While this was not an area identified by the accreditation team or an intended outcome at the beginning, it became apparent that each person was coming to the table with his or her own philosophies. It became an area of focus so teachers would understand that it was okay to argue with each other based on philosophies, and though they differed, they could make progress working on the same project. The third area of focus was to create virtual space for teachers to share their practices.

Capturing impact on student learning specific to engagement is difficult. There is no concrete information for the school other than what teachers report from the classroom. Teachers within the school agreed to promote student ownership of their own learning process. Along with this concept was the understanding that to build relationships there must be trust. Teachers looked for meaningful moments of learning versus time online. There was an understanding that it's the students' course, and the teacher is facilitating.

As a staff, teachers build collegiality. There is an openness where one will model and share, and then the group works together to create learning activities. There is an effort to obtain input and help others see a different way (e.g., method, strategy, style). As a system, collaboration time was provided on a weekly basis. Each department or grade level was provided 45 minutes per week. The committee provides monthly themes such as "First Day Classroom Culture."

Daniele recalls her superintendent when she was working in Germany. He stated that she should "go as fast as you can and as slow as you must." This stood out to Daniele as she was in the process of switching schools, and it gave her time to reflect and grow as a professional. As an online teacher, there are different, small moments of success. She recognizes what she wants may not match her colleagues' needs, and a great moment for them should be celebrated, as it takes small steps in succession to get to where you want to go. As teacher leaders, we need to celebrate the successes of staff and students alike.

Daniele shares that the best preparation she received was unintentional. Her master's in student personnel administration falls outside of the field of education. When she entered education as a new teacher, she felt isolated, defeated, and tired. Her mentor recommended she explore higher education residential life, and she created a transition program from high school to a four-year institution. However, her husband was deployed to Germany, and there were no universities there for her to continue to work in this capacity.

Noncognitive successes were celebrated through avenues such as algebra, and through a colleague she observed the changing path of a student. This trusted colleague became a co-chair, and both taught algebra. Trial and error was an essential driving factor to the success of change, and having a trusted colleague was key.

As one teacher among 4.6 million (National Center for Education Statistics, 2018, p. 53) across the United States, serving as a teacher leader is a humbling experience. Goals change over time, but one factor that has surfaced as instrumental is a strong sense of confidence: confidence in who you are and what you do because you know you have students at the heart of every aspect of your work and every decision. Confidence includes the ability to stand up and challenge so as not to be seen as arrogant, but to leave fear behind.

Areas of strength for Daniele include building a professional network to tap into and the willingness to put herself in a position of vulnerability. Sharing her own failures is not easy but serves as a great learning tool for herself and others alike. Growth can be confirmed through understanding of research and data. Other areas of strength include always focusing on relationships with students and the ability to build on quiet moments of the journey.

Areas of focus for Daniele include challenging her own thinking and building up reflective practice. A third area of focus is to be more intentional about reflection and to allow people to struggle through an uncomfortable situation, being careful that it's not at the expense of the student.

At the time of this case study, Daniele's husband was deployed to the Middle East. She was in the final stages of completing her dissertation and felt great about being a teacher and serving as a teacher leader. Her passion for teaching would not be lost as she continued to grow and change, but would be nurtured to take her in directions she might not even be aware of. Daniele's mantra is, "Be in the present."

RONALD TOWNS, ACADEMIC DEAN OF MATHEMATICS, LEADERSHIP PUBLIC SCHOOLS, OAKLAND, CALIFORNIA

This case study is about an experienced teacher leader and urban educator who shares how a new curricular initiative can challenge an experienced teacher leader. Experienced teacher leaders bring the capacity to focus on the essential elements needed for effective, meaningful change. Ron Towns began his urban, public school teaching career as department chair in a turnaround high school in Chicago. Then he moved to California to continue his commitment to urban youth and teacher leadership. In his ninth year of teaching, Ron was hired as the academic dean of mathematics in Leadership Public Schools (LPS), a public charter high school in Oakland, California.

Ron's new position combined department chair responsibilities with instructional coaching and teaching. Like many schools in California, LPS was moving to the Common Core State Standards (CCSS). Also at that time, approximately one in five students was performing at proficient or higher on the state mathematics exam, California Assessment of Student Performance and Progress (CAASPP). In addition, Ron was the only mathematics teacher in his new department who had prior experiences with the CCSS, and he viewed the reason for his hiring as being to help the school shift to Common Core and improve mathematics instruction.

The public charter school where Ron became the mathematics academic dean is situated on the same campus in East Oakland as the larger public high school. The charter, however, has a nonselective student enrollment of 400 students and provides students with the college preparatory coursework required to apply to a public university in California. This preparatory coursework is known as the A-G requirements.

The student body is predominantly Latinx (90%) and African American (10%), with more than 90% of the students qualifying for free/reduced lunch. Approximately a third of the student body is English Language Learners, and 8–9% of the students are newcomers to the United States, mostly from Latin America and Spanish speaking. While performance on the state mathematics exams is low, with 18% of students scoring proficient or higher, 65% of the students score proficient or higher on the English language arts exam.

Ron's credentials and experiences were well suited for this leadership position. Not only had he previously led mathematics departments and coached teachers, but he had spent a year teaching in Spain and was proficient in Spanish. He had earned a master's degree in teacher leadership and an administrative credential. Although he was still early in his career, with nine years of experience, this exceeded the experience of other mathematics teachers in his new department: one third-year teacher, three second-year teachers, and one first-year teacher.

Ron's overarching goal for his first year as academic dean of mathematics was for every teacher to know the major work standards for CCSS-Mathematics and to clearly identify what proficient student work would look like. He believed that if they accomplished this goal, then students would show gains on the common assessments, which were end-of-unit tests adopted across all the charter high schools. Ron also believed that working toward 80% mastery on work standards would translate into better state exam performance. However, he did not believe that focusing on student performance data was sufficient. As a teacher leader, his understanding was that reaching these goals would require having relational trust with colleagues and not taking that for granted; a clear focus that made sense to people about an instructional practice and area where there were specific action steps that they were all taking together; and clear metrics to show whether the teachers were getting better and the kids were getting better as a result.

Ron and one of the other mathematics teachers, Arthur, attended a conference on the CCSS-Mathematics prior to the beginning of the school year. However, Ron did not immediately initiate major changes in the department. Rather, he worked within the existing structure, described as a culture around having an instructional coach.

Therefore, as the new mathematics instructional coach, Ron began to get to know each teacher. He explained: "That was a lot of building relational trust with them. So, when I would do coaching, I would meet with people one-on-one and really try to get to know them as people and also show that I cared about their professional growth." Ron spent the first four months building relational trust and seeing his colleagues teach so he was familiar with them as mathematics teachers. The team had also seen Ron teach. "They knew I could teach, so I built 'street credit' with them," Ron continued.

During the same time period, from August to December, there was regularly scheduled time for the team to meet to establish common goals and discuss the CCSS-Mathematics. Ron used this time to really focus on instruction through coaching and did a lot of department level work, asking questions like "What is our vision as a math team?" The team looked at students' current data and where they were trying to go. There was a lot of building community, and some out-of-classroom outings like an escape room and wine tasting. Previously there were five math teachers but no math team, no math department. Now they built a team.

Ron found that Arthur was a valuable resource. Not only had Arthur attended the CCSS-Math conference with Ron, but he was the most likely to be skeptical about new ideas. Ron saw this as a positive:

> He was like my thermometer, so I would go to him and ask, *What did you think about this meeting?* And in advance of a meeting, I would talk through some of my ideas about our PD sessions because if he is on board, then everyone is going to be on board. And he had gone to the conference with me, so he had this insight to help lead some of the work. He had also been at the school longer than the rest of the team, so he had been frustrated with the way things had been done and was eager for a change.

Being in his colleagues' classrooms as an instructional coach gave Ron important insights. For example, he began to ask the teachers about checking for student understanding. He would work with teachers on their major work standards and discuss assessment questions like, "What would proficient look like on this standard?" Ron's coaching varied by teacher experience and need. The first-year teacher needed more support with classroom management along with giving feedback and checking for understanding, while the other teachers needed to align their assessment practices to the increased rigor of the CCSS-Mathematics. Ron's coaching was differentiated, but he made sure they all came together with a common focus.

In January Ron led the team through what he called the first official cycle of inquiry with an instructional focus. Ron admits that as they began the inquiry, he was very directive in his leadership, determining that the focus of the inquiry would be on checking for understanding and giving feedback. He explained that as a team they needed to improve at checking for understanding of student learning in the moment and giving feedback to students during class or the next day. He chose this focus because during the first semester of coaching, he had observed a greater need for checking if students had learned during daily lessons and knew that changing this practice would improve student learning and test performance. Ron described his approach as scaffolded:

> First through coaching, I worked on [strategies] like "let's give an exit ticket," "let's do a class reflection or summary," those in-the-class practices that summarized the learning. So then second semester since we had done the work, I was like "How can we amplify the work we have already done?" So, I brought in assessment for learning practices, assessment in the moment and giving feedback to kids as our focus.

While the entire school used inquiry cycles, the mathematics department's inquiry was unique in two important ways: (a) they focused on instructional practices in addition to student outcomes, and (b) their measures of effectiveness were student performance on major work standards rather than grades.

The inquiry cycle (Cushman, 1999) began with collecting baseline data on both student outcomes and teacher practice. Step 2 was selecting an instructional focus to improve student outcomes. Step 3 gave everyone time to practice their chosen strategies, followed by Step 4, which involved coaching observations with feedback. Finally, the team regrouped to examine how the students were doing as a result of their cycle. Then the cycle repeated.

To begin the very first cycle of inquiry, Ron explained to the team how he had observed improvements on checking for understanding at the end class but asked that they challenge each other to assess by living in the moment. This meant that teachers would be able to check for understanding and give feedback during lessons to improve student learning. Ron brought in some research to discuss and explained the inquiry cycle steps they would take.

The first step in the inquiry cycle was collecting baseline data on where students were and where the team was with their teaching practices in terms of checking for understanding. Ron pulled student data from the learning management system and shared the end-of-unit tests progress by standard, so everyone could see where they were starting.

Then he introduced the need to collect baseline data on their teaching practices. "An important part of gathering baseline data was getting teachers to see where they were as adult practitioners and ask *Where are we starting?*" Ron found this reflective part to be tricky, so he led them through peer observations, where they observed but did not give feedback to one another, just collected data on "How are we checking for understanding so far?" "What are the ways we are checking for understanding currently?" and "Do we check for understanding?"

The team met and debriefed after the peer observations. Team members saw that they did some checks for understanding but needed to develop better strategies and needed more strategies. Another finding from the peer observations was that there was a lot of checking for understanding through questioning, but often using low-level questions (e.g., procedure-based or leading questions). The team decided they wanted to focus on other ways to check for understanding and on how to ask tiered questions.

Ron purchased a book on checking for understanding and shared some of the chapters (e.g., one chapter on questioning, several chapters on specific strategies). The teachers chose which strategies they wanted to try. During this phase of the inquiry cycle, every time the team met, they would share progress on implementing strategies and teach each other how to use them. In addition, the teachers would discuss how to build strategies into their lesson plans. Then through coaching, Ron would give individual feedback on how well they were implementing the new strategies by providing data on how the students were responding to the checks for understanding.

The mathematics team definitely made progress. They saw their students' state test scores go up 10 percentage points that year. At the last meeting of the school year, the teachers listed all the strategies they had learned to check for understanding. Ron could see the difference in his colleagues' classrooms: they implemented more strategies more effectively. However, the progress was not easy, as Ron explained:

> It was a lot of work, getting everyone on the same page. I think that is what is hardest, making sure everyone understands *Why are we doing this? What are we trying to do?* So, it is clear. When you try to change instruction, it is very easy for people to do what they want if it is not focused, or for people to not do anything at all if it is too micromanaged.

As a teacher leader, Ron described the balance he had to provide: "Where are the spaces where I need to be directive as the leader of this team, and where are the spaces where giving choice would actually help? I need to know each teacher well enough to think about these questions and plan."

Ron did not experience resistance to his proposed changes from his math department colleagues. However, he acknowledged that he was aware of possible areas of pushback. For example, he described how carefully he approached the peer observations: "We didn't have a culture of giving peer-to-peer feedback, which is a whole different layer of emotion. I wanted to build a culture of observing each other but . . . kept it safe." He also acknowledged that his team was surprised by the focus on their practice and not just the student learning to which he responded: "I was like 'yeah, if we're not doing something effectively then why would the kids improve?' I think that was a huge thing and the relational trust is key to that process."

Ron said he always learns alongside leading, including adding more strategies for checking for comprehension and improving his effectiveness in questioning. However, this leadership experience presented some new learning at the building level. As mentioned previously, all departments were using the inquiry cycle to improve outcomes, but only the mathematics department was focusing on teaching practices and not using grades as student outcome measures. At the school-wide leadership meetings, Ron found himself in the uncomfortable position of having to explain both his team's success and why they were doing their own thing:

> We were the only ones doing this cycle of inquiry—different from everyone else—so we went against the grain. But our kids and teachers achieved more. It was not necessarily viewed as team players at the school level. How do you not show up at the whole school meeting being too cool for the school?

Ron saw the mathematic team's inquiry growth as the teachers' getting good at research-based instructional practices regardless of where they worked versus having the attitude "let's just look at how our kids are doing and try different things." When it came to looking at student data, all other departments examined grades. Ron readily acknowledged that in a high-stakes high school environment people care about grades, but he felt he had to resist conforming.

Even the principal had pushed examining grades, and she initially thought that Ron viewed grades as unimportant. Ron clarified what he was saying: "If only 18% of kids are passing the [state test], which isn't the end all/be all, but it is only 18%, and most of our kids are passing our classes, there's something wrong. We need to actually look at what they are learning."

Ron summarized his lessons learned in teacher leadership: "I learned that I have to make sure my language is clear in those other spaces. I need to be clear about what we're doing and representing us well. I'm not Ron Towns, mathematics teacher or instructional coach. I am Ron Towns, leader of this mathematics effort that is different and [I need to] attend to how people perceive that."

LILLY BRUCESTER, SPECIAL EDUCATION TEACHER, CENTRAL WISCONSIN

In this case study, Lilly Brucester (a pseudonym), a high school special education teacher in Wisconsin, discusses a variety of teacher leader roles, emphasizing that for her, the role of teacher mentor has been most impactful. As the teacher shortage receives greater attention across the nation, more and more conversations about teacher leadership and the impact it could have on the teacher shortage are taking place.

Lilly provides cross-categorical support and services to grades 9–12 in a public high school in a district identified as urban. The district's student population is primarily white (69.2%) with 16% students with disabilities, 9% English Language Learners, and 40% economically disadvantaged (under $25,000 in a household of three). Lilly's school mirrors the district, with a slightly higher level of 45% students from families identified as economically disadvantaged.

The district reports that 65.8% of its students meet state achievement expectations, and it has an 83.9 % graduation rate. In all, there are three high schools, a specialized high school, four middle schools, and sixteen elementary schools that make up the district in which Lilly teaches. There are also several charter schools.

Lilly explained that teacher leadership takes on many different roles in her district and added that teachers in her district need 40 hours of professional development each year. "This is the highest that any district in the state requires—some don't require any," Lilly stated. One of the roles that teacher leaders take on in Lilly's district is that of providing professional development. Lilly clarified that teachers were able to offer professional development by sending a proposal to the district, obtaining approval, and then putting their offerings on the district calendar. Offerings varied from teachers with special expertise to a book study.

Lilly has also served on district curriculum committees for mathematics and communication arts. Serving on district curriculum committees was another role that teacher leaders took on in Lilly's district. This role was unpaid and for teachers in special education. There was no application process, as special education representation was a highly sought after commodity in her district. A special education teacher who wanted to be on the committee was automatically selected. District staff ran the curriculum committees, and they also set the time lines to align with curricular decisions that had to go before the school board for approval and requisitions.

Teachers also serve in leadership roles through implementation of special district initiatives. Lilly shared:

> The initiative committees often take anyone in special education because it's such a high area of need and burnout, you just don't see a lot of special education teachers at the high school level involved in extra committees, initiatives or events.

One initiative Lilly worked on was Positive Behavior Intervention Support (PBIS). In addition to a lot of meetings with other faculty members, initiatives like these often involved special training using a train-the-trainer model. Teacher leaders were then involved in working on district implementation plans and training other teachers. Lilly noted, "The challenge of this work is that not everyone is always philosophically aligned, and that part of the training is not included."

Most recently Lilly was invited to participate in her district's Trauma Successful Schools initiative, which developed in response to two recent suicides in the district. This initiative also brought support from the state and a representative from the state board, who met regularly with the district leadership team.

A more formal teacher leader program was the mentoring program. Lilly explained that mentoring was a paid position for which teachers applied. "Every new teacher and every teacher new to our district gets a mentor for a certain amount of time." In this district someone who is brand-new gets a mentor for three years. In each subsequent year, they meet a little less often.

To be a mentor in Lilly's district, one has to go through special mentor training that is offered at the district level. Lilly had gone through mentor training and had been a mentor several times, both in her building and in other schools within the district. Lilly clarified, "In the first year, mentors are required to have weekly contact, a formal visit once a month, and an observation once a month. The mentors are given time to do both the visits and the meetings. In the second year, mentors have contact every other week. The observations drop to twice a quarter." Lilly shared that if situations arose, the mentor could arrange additional meetings.

Evaluation is completely separate from mentoring. The district uses the Danielson Framework (2011) for teacher evaluation, and the mentors can help teachers understand the model. For example, the mentors were able to help their mentees understand each of the domains and pointed out examples of particular instances of Danielson objectives when they saw their mentees using them in an observed or discussed lesson. "The mentor/mentee relationship is very confidential," said Lilly. "I have the same evaluator as some of my mentees so I would not tell my supervisor anything about how the teacher I was mentoring was doing and betray that confidence." Lilly did go on to say, however, that sometimes the evaluator came to the mentors with specific requests for things to work on or talk to a mentee about, and that was appropriate.

While it was not always the case, mentors in Lilly's district were able to get together twice a year. This provided ongoing support to the mentors in addition to the training they had undertaken in the district. Similarly, the new teachers also had opportunities to get together and talk about the mentoring program and their experiences. New teachers also had the opportunity to request a new mentor.

The mentor role is a three-year commitment. "In year 3," Lilly explained, "I could get a new mentee, but it wouldn't be a brand new teacher as the time commitment is very intense with new teachers." Lilly also explained that the stipends the mentors received were contractual and were negotiated by the union.

Lilly believes that every job needs mentors because one never comes into a job knowing everything. There are always things that are done a little differently based on the school or district or that are new. In all new jobs one needs someone to talk to. It needs to be someone who can be at mentees' beck and call so they can be the best version of themselves, and so the institution or organization can be successful. The goal of mentoring in education is that new teachers (a) gain understanding about their new positions and its ins and outs, (b) develop confidence, (c) are able to focus on building relationships with students and parents, (d) are able to design and implement instruction, (e) develop successful students, and (f) engage to the point where they never want to leave.

The mentors in Lilly's district use SMART (Specific, Measurable, Assignable, Relevant, and Time-based) goals and really try to focus on their mentees, what the mentees may want to achieve and do, and how to get them there. The mentors help them work with My Learning Plan, a district-based program that teachers use to keep track of professional development (PD) hours, their student and teacher learning outcomes, and action plans. Lilly described the process in this way: "We log our hours using this tool and the district logs into each to keep track of our hours and so on. Every three years we have a summary year and we have to have 120 hours." In Lilly's district, they review teacher plans and submit them to the state. The teachers' Danielson goals are located in the same tool. Teachers also have to submit their reviews of sexual harassment, blood-borne pathogens, and other trainings.

"The biggest barrier for teacher leaders in this endeavor is timing," divulged Lilly. "I don't like to be out of my classroom as I have to have a substitute and they don't come in with the background that they need to carry out my plans." For Lilly, that feels like lost instructional time with her students, and she feels terrible about anything that negatively affects student learning. Lilly tends to meet her mentees outside of school hours and only does observations during the school day.

"The success of the mentoring project," continued Lilly, "requires full-on cooperation from the building principal. That was never a problem in our district as there was such great buy-in from the board and superintendent down." Lilly also admitted that the new teachers also had to be really open and ready for this hard work and reflection. "What's really hard," confessed Lilly, "is when the mentee thinks all is well and it isn't!" Lilly added that sometimes the issues were challenging. For example, Lilly had a colleague whose mentee was bad-mouthing other teachers. The mentee just didn't see the problem and wouldn't stop. "Well," said Lilly, "sometimes you do have to go back and let administrators step in, but that is rare."

Lilly believes that mentoring was the teacher leader accomplishment that had the greatest impact, as it affected the quality of student instruction, staff and parent relationships, and teacher success. She aspired to the idea that one only returns to do things that one feels good about, so investing in teacher success was integral to student success and, therefore, teacher retention. "I think it makes me a better teacher and leader, too," Lilly reflected, adding, "Our school and our parents benefit, too."

While Lilly engaged in many teacher leader roles, she remarked that she never really thought of herself as a teacher leader. Lilly shared, "I'm always learning something new about our practice, about myself and especially about conflict—especially at the high school level." Lilly thinks that a lot of the places where she is providing leadership are things that good teachers should just be doing. Lilly continued, "I don't do all these things by myself, either, so I think that makes me think maybe I'm not a teacher leader—just a really good teacher."

Asked about her five-year plan, Lilly said she would like to be more involved in transition programs in special education, perhaps at the hospital level. "I don't really want to go into administration—I love teaching!"

SUMMARY

This chapter emphasized the accomplishments of teacher leaders serving at the high school level. Their investment in learning how to involve students and putting energy in where it counts impacted student learning in various ways. With growing emphasis on high-stakes assessments, these teacher leaders at the high school level involved students in their own learning so they would take ownership and know their destinations. "The research is clear: Students learn and achieve more when they are deeply involved in the process of classroom assessment, and teachers who use quality classroom assessment practices have more students learning and achieving at higher levels" (Davies, 2007, p. 52). The positive relationships among engagement, involvement, and ownership are evident with teachers in coaching and mentoring relationships as well through the highest level of mentoring: Work with Me. At this level, the mentee works with the mentor as the expert who offers hands-on, side-by-side guidance to learn and strengthen skills and build capacity in others (Strike & Nickelsen, 2011, p. 4).

REFLECTIVE QUESTIONS AND APPLICATION

1. Reflect on the leadership of each teacher highlighted in this chapter. Place him/her on the rubrics provided in the figures near the beginning of the chapter and justify your placement.
2. Self-assessment: reflecting on your own experiences and actions, place yourself on the rubrics provided in the figures near the beginning of this chapter. What area(s) of strength stand out, and what might you do to improve or obtain additional experience?
3. Identify the vision and purpose of the work of each teacher leader.
4. What were some of the challenges in translating each teacher leader's vision into operational terms? What alternatives or changes might you recommend? Is this something you have, or something that could work in your own setting? If not, what changes would need to be made for it to work in your own setting?
5. What contributes to each leader's success?
6. What aspects of each story resonated with you, and what did you learn from each story that might help in your own practice?
7. What observations have you made in looking at the leadership highlighted in this chapter, specific to teacher leadership at the high school level, compared to that shared in other chapters? Would you say teacher leadership is easier to plan and implement within the high school setting? Why or why not?

REFERENCES

Cushman, K. (1999). *The cycle of inquiry and action: Essential learning communities.* Coalition of Essential Schools. Retrieved from http://essentialschools.org/horace-issues/the-cycle-of-inquiry-and-action-essential-learning-communities/

Danielson, C. (2011). *The framework for teaching evaluation instrument*. Princeton, NJ: The Danielson Group.

Davies, A. (2007). Involving students in the classroom assessment process. In D. Reeves (Ed.), *Ahead of the curve: The power of assessment to transform teaching and learning*. Bloomington, IN: Solution Tree Press.

Strike, K., Fitzsimmons, J. & Hornberger, R. (2019). *Identifying and growing internal leaders: A framework for effective teacher leadership*. Lanham, MD: Rowman & Littlefield.

Strike, K., & Nickelsen, J. (2011). *Mentoring the educational leader: A practical framework for success*. Lanham, MD: Rowman & Littlefield.

US Department of Education, National Center for Education Statistics. (2018). *Digest of education statistics, 2016* (p. 53) (NCES 2017-094).

Chapter Six

Teacher Leadership
of K–12 Specialists

This chapter focuses on teacher leadership of K–12 Specialists. In the case studies provided in this chapter you will read about Alisa M. Strike, an elementary level music teacher, who provides individualized education to autistic students. You will also read about Adam Mullis, a middle school physical education teacher whose leadership with the FitnessBowl has impacted the district. This chapter also highlights the leadership of Pearl Stanton, a speech pathologist serving students at multiple levels who also serves as an officer in the teacher's union. Finally, we share the case study of Charlotte Brenner, who serves as an elementary level learning support teacher.

The case studies in this chapter are examples of Domains 3, Instructional Leadership, and 4, Advocacy in *Identifying and Growing Internal Leaders: A Framework for Effective Teacher Leadership* (Strike, Fitzsimmons, & Hornberger, 2019). As you read each of the case studies, consider "3c: Provides an effective instructional program" (see figure 6.1) and "4c: Supports local initiatives" (see figure 6.2).

Reflect on the leadership of each teacher highlighted in this chapter. Place the case study on the rubric in the figures and justify your placement. Examine the impact of the teacher leader's decisions and the opportunities afforded in their context. Consider successes, alternatives, or changes you might recommend as an observer, and possibilities for your own setting.

3c: Provides an effective instructional program	Level of Performance			
Element	Ineffective	Initiating	Developing	Effective
Advocates for instruction that supports the needs for all learners	Does not advocate for instruction that supports the needs of all learners	Inconsistently advocates for instruction that supports the needs of all learners	Consistently advocates for instruction that supports the needs of all learners	Creates, implements and consistently advocates for instruction that supports the needs of all learners

Figure 6.1. Partial rubric for Framework for Effective Teacher Leadership (3c).
Copyright © Strike, Fitzsimmons, & Hornberger, 2019.

4c: Supports local initiatives	Level of Performance			
Element	Ineffective	Initiating	Developing	Effective
Collaborates with stakeholders to ensure learner growth and advancement of the profession	Fails to collaborate with stakeholders to ensure learner growth and advancement of the profession	Attempts to collaborate with stakeholders to ensure learner growth and advancement of the profession	Actively collaborates with stakeholders to ensure learner growth and advancement of the profession	Develops a collaborative culture with stakeholders to ensure learner growth and advancement of the profession

Figure 6.2. Partial rubric for Framework for Effective Teacher Leadership (4c).
Copyright © Strike, Fitzsimmons, & Hornberger, 2019.

ALISA M. STRIKE, MUSIC TEACHER, FROST ELEMENTARY SCHOOL, HILLSBOROUGH COUNTY, RIVERVIEW, FLORIDA

This case study focuses on one teacher's journey to meet autistic students where they are to provide each the opportunity to receive the education he/she deserves. Through a quest of self-improvement by a music teacher who encountered a new group of students with needs she didn't feel trained to meet, her journey led to helping other teachers through district-wide training.

Frost Elementary School is located in suburban Hillsborough County, Florida, approximately 10 minutes outside of Tampa. It houses students in grades K–5, with grades 1–5 participating in music classes. It is a Type I, top tier Title I school with over 600 students. The student population is 38% black, 37% Hispanic, 16% white, and 9% other (including bi- or multiracial).

Alisa serves as a music teacher and teacher leader at Frost Elementary, where she has chosen to teach for over nine years. She points out that there is always room for improvement, regardless of how long one has been teaching. One must renew the desire to learn. Alisa encourages others to step out of their comfort zone, be flexible, and embrace change.

In Hillsborough County, formal roles for teacher leaders include lead teachers, peer mentors, and teacher talent developers. These are roles for which the interested person must apply and be interviewed. Informal roles for teacher leaders include transportation assistant, scheduling assistant, and team leader within the area of specialty. These roles are filled by person(s) with experience in such areas.

In 2010 Frost Elementary School moved from a focus on trainable mentally handicapped (TMH) students to autism spectrum disorder (ASD). Alisa served as the music teacher, serving grades 1–5. As she worked with the ASD students, she felt inadequate and questioned how she could better meet the students' needs.

Alisa recognized that this was an area for which she hadn't been prepared. She reached out to obtain additional resources, including a course offered through Shriner's Hospital, University of South Florida (USF), and ASD training online. She collaborated with teachers who specialized in working with students with autism and a teacher who had received her master's in music therapy. Signs and symptoms became easier to identify, but Alisa questioned how to set up her classroom to best meet the needs of the students she was entrusted to serve.

Alisa willingly asked others for suggestions and was open to trial and error in her own music classroom. She collaborated with general education teachers and piggybacked with ASD classroom teachers to create procedures that were more consistent. This took a few years to learn and then implement but became recognized by her colleagues. After five years of continuous collaboration with the music therapist, Alisa became much more comfortable with practices and procedures. Student success is evident, and she is being recognized by fellow teachers.

There are data that show evidence of change. The most significant is through performance. Observations confirm students in grades K, 1, and 2 find transition difficult. Prompting is needed to move students through activities, and patience is essential. However, by the time students reach the fourth and fifth grades, they serve as student leaders within the classroom. A rubric is in place for students to be self-accountable. Hillsborough County requires a district assessment of students in music, and students with ASD are not exempt.

While the goal for this project was self-improvement by a music teacher who encountered a new group of students with needs she didn't feel trained to meet, her journey led to helping other teachers through district-wide training.

Alisa's colleague who specializes in music therapy brings the head knowledge of when, where, why, and kinesthetics. Alisa provides practical knowledge and effective implementation. Strategies, tools, and resources are effectively shared with colleagues, such as a visual calendar, ordering music that aligns with topics learned in their classroom, a parachute to practice purposeful movement, and carpet squares to provide a magic island of personal space.

One of the greatest challenges is that the budget for the music program housing the students with ASD and general education students is $75 per year. That amount is to cover the 500 students Alisa supports in her music classroom, including printing music and choir programs for performances. The music program is provided five reams of paper and one ink cartridge for the year. In September of each year, teachers can apply for Florida Teacher Classroom Supply Assistance, which is a project of the legislature that allocates funds to each Florida teacher to help offset the cost of supplemental materials and supplies. The amount varies based on funds appropriated and full-time student enrollment. Alisa receives $274 and must keep receipts for four years.

An additional challenge is the unpredictability of the students. There is a wide range on the autism spectrum, and every child on the spectrum is different. For example, some are verbal, some nonverbal; some are potty trained, some are not; some can read and some cannot. Those who are higher functioning are included in general education through FAPE (Free Appropriate Public Education). However, a student who is moved into the general education classroom may still show signs and behaviors of ASD, including social, communication, and behavioral challenges. The challenge is then differentiating the lesson for the student(s) with ASD. This calls for the teacher to anticipate and respond to the variety of student needs in the classroom in order to provide maximum learning.

There are several outcomes for this case study. First is the identification, implementation, and evaluation of strategies to be successful in the music classroom. Second is the identification and use of manipulatives specific to each student's needs. For example, some students like vibration, while it disturbs others, so magic ears are made available. Others might need something in their hands to expend the energy.

A third outcome is to generate and encourage student leaders, just like their general education counterparts. Students with ASD can lead in creative movement, work the visual calendar, pass out and pick up supplies, and give directions. Finally, and most important, is to focus on student success. Being purposeful with students, such as pitch match, purposeful movement, and performance through instruments, provides students the opportunity to be successful.

Alisa has had a great impact on her colleagues. Classroom teachers are thankful for the guidance and support she provides to meet the needs of their students. Strategies and information are often not offered or not easily found; however, Alisa is willing to dig for answers. Because of this, she has received Excellence in Education nominations from her peers. They value her input specific to what she does in her classroom and how it connects to theirs.

As a school, the staff believe students need to receive the education they deserve. For Alisa in the music room, this includes vibrations and hands-on tailoring of music education. The district has taken notice, and Alisa has been invited to provide district-wide in-services focused on students with ASD in the music classroom. Her support has provided avenues for autistic students to participate in district-wide choir through the use of audio files the students could memorize when they weren't able to read music. Through social interaction, their inclusion opened the door for other students.

The greatest observable impact has been on families. For example, one family has three of four children on the spectrum. The parent is exhausted, but when she sees her children perform in the music productions there is a sense of pride in their successes. Serving as an advocate is a regular occurrence, as several families in the school have multiple siblings on the spectrum. In one case, a parent fought for her child to attend choir in the transfer school, and Alisa was able to assist with procedures to allow the incoming music teacher to adapt.

Alisa identifies her strengths as flexibility, the willingness to take advice (constructive feedback), and the recognition of others' abilities (build capacity in others). She recognizes it's not about her. She's open to new ideas and moves out of her comfort zone. She recognizes she has a lot to learn yet, but that it's the parents and students who benefit. Alisa reminds us that sometimes it's through lack of preparation that we can determine what we need and go after it. The needs within the school and the willingness to help are core to a teacher leader. The phrase teacher leaders use is, "How can I help you?"

Alisa informally serves on the transportation team in her current school, is involved in scheduling, has previously served as the team leader for specialists in her building, and serves as a directing teacher for music interns. Beyond service to the school, she has proven she can recognize and meet each child where he/she is, provide procedures that connect to experiences outside of her classroom, and advocate for students to receive the education and enrichment they deserve.

Exploration of opportunities would best capture where Alisa is in her career as a teacher leader. She anticipates that she will remain in her current district. There is a willingness to explore other roles and responsibilities under the umbrella of teacher leadership, such as a peer mentor or lead teacher. However, budget cuts have been deep throughout the district, and teacher leader positions have been on the receiving end of the slashes.

ADAM MULLIS, PHYSICAL EDUCATION TEACHER, CRAYTON MIDDLE SCHOOL, RICHLAND COUNTY, COLUMBIA, SOUTH CAROLINA

This case study focuses on one teacher's journey to bring students to an awareness of the benefits of being healthy and to change a school culture to one that celebrates health and fitness. Through this teacher's FitnessBowl program, students who might not be athletic are celebrated for their focus and growth in health and fitness.

Richland County School District One (Richland 1) is a public school district located in South Carolina. Within the county, there are 28 elementary schools, 9 middle schools, 8 high schools, an alternative school, a school specific for special needs, and a middle college serving grades 11–12. The district mission is transforming lives through education, empowering all students to achieve their potential and dreams.

Crayton Middle School is the largest middle school in the district and serves approximately 1,200 students in grades 6–8. The school is diverse in nature. Demographics show 40% of the students are African American, 50% Caucasian, and 10% other. The special education population is 11.3%, and over 45% of the students enrolled receive some type of state assistance (Medicaid, Supplemental Nutrition Assistance Program [SNAP], Temporary Assistance to Families with Children [TANF], foster, or homeless). Over 49% of the students are served through the gifted and talented program, and 30% are receiving high school credit while in middle school.

The school continues to receive a rating of excellent from the South Carolina Department of Education. The mission of Crayton Middle School is to uphold high expectations and positive relationships to increase the achievement of all stakeholders. The school encourages a strong sense of excellence through the tagline, "Expect the Best, Give the Best, Be the Best!"

The role of the teacher leader tends to be informal in Richland 1. While formal training is offered for specific teacher leader tasks such as serving as a mentor, teachers rise as leaders from the classroom based on need specific to one's role. To serve as a lead teacher, safety evaluator, or mentor calls for specific training but not a specific number of years of experience. Such opportunities often come from recommendations from the assistant principal or principal. Opportunities to serve may include committee work, serving as a mentor, or assisting with state evaluation.

Adam Mullis is a health and physical education (PE) teacher. He serves as a co-lead teacher in addition to his role as a classroom teacher. His assigned duties as a co-lead are specific to providing professional development at the beginning and in the middle of the school year, with some curriculum work during the summer. Adam is president elect of the South Carolina Association for Physical Education and Sport. He has assisted with the planning, implementation, and sustainment of a district-wide fitness competition called FitnessBowl, health week at the school level, and national recognition with Healthier Generation.

As a teacher leader, Adam advanced the movement toward a healthier environment and stepped up to promote, encourage, and celebrate health awareness. While this role is informal, it has impacted the community, district, school, colleagues, and students. It opened the door to talk with administrators about health awareness and was instrumental in changing the culture of the school.

In the case of the FitnessBowl, it wasn't a matter of creating something new, but of extending something beyond its current end and tailoring it to the needs of the children served. The 28 elementary schools in Richland 1 have a concept like FitnessBowl. As a teacher leader, Adam saw a need and approached his elementary colleagues to extend and intensify the elementary version to a middle school version. There are nine middle schools, eight of which participate depending on the year. At the time of this case study, the FitnessBowl was in its third year at the middle school level.

The original idea derived from the use of FitnessGram® MP. There seemed to be no reason and no purpose for it other than that it was a requirement, so Adam decided to try to make it more fun and purposeful. The main purpose or inspiration of this idea comes from a way to make the state-required Fitness-Gram more fun. Adam's intent was to improve the health of students in a more meaningful and impactful way that his students would enjoy.

The FitnessGram test battery assesses health-related fitness components: aerobic capacity; body composition; and muscular strength, endurance, and flexibility. Activity assessments are included for step or minute challenges, physical activity behaviors, and overall activity levels to provide teachers with a variety of ways to promote physical activity to students (Cooper Institute, 2018).

Adam met with his colleagues at the elementary schools to obtain foresight and create a middle school version with age-appropriate activities. It was helpful to talk to elementary people because they were willing to help, and they could foresee additional issues. Other teachers were very helpful, as were administrators with processes such as obtaining a building, getting microphones, or setting up security (district level). Adam brainstormed with a district advisor and translated what was done at the elementary level into what was needed at the middle school with the goal to improve the health of children. He then e-mailed each school with information.

Adam and another teacher came up with a game plan (an action plan but less formal) that had a step-by-step process of every little detail they could think of that they might need to cover. They wrote every detail they could come up with on a whiteboard, identifying needs and then who could cover that detail to even out the load and make it as successful as possible, since all involved were also serving as full-time teachers. Many meetings specific to processes followed, taking place outside of the school day.

The specifics for the FitnessBowl were a group effort. By law, each school is required to participate in FitnessGram, but only the top students can participate in FitnessBowl. As Adam saw it, the cool thing was as the bar is raised, all students' fitness scores increase. Each school selects a team and attends a Saturday event that features push-ups, standing long jump, an agility test, and so on. Each school competes for the best score within a scoring system. Adam is charged with getting the building and overall, everything that happens. Other schools are charged with issuing tickets, getting equipment, providing activities while scores are calculated, obtaining volunteers (running scores, nurses, athletic trainers), and getting trophies. Adam acknowledged it's a lot of people doing a lot of little things to help this event come together.

One challenge Adam faced was running the event for the first time. Having a vision of what something could be and then coming to the realization that it's just not there is difficult. As Adam pointed out:

> [T]hen you must consider that it's the first year. As the teacher leader, you must sell people on an event that's not where we want it to be yet. There's an understanding that the FitnessBowl is a good thing for kids, and they'll get excited about fitness which is the whole point of PE. However, it's challenging to get people to understand that it's not going to happen right now. Changing some events in the 2nd and 3rd year brought the event to a level where it could be, so going from Year 1 to Year 2 was moving from night to day.

Intended outcomes of the FitnessBowl were to increase best practices with health and PE; increase FitnessGram scores; and promote health and PE to students, parents, and schools. The FitnessBowl had support from the get-go.

Statistically, teachers look at FitnessGram each year. During the years of FitnessBowl, the average of kids in the healthy fitness zone, specifically in the pacer and especially in cardiovascular endurance, has increased by 2% per year. Looking from the pretest, that number is higher than ever. It's on an upper trend, and higher than it's ever been for the school.

The culture has changed. Kids don't complain about running anymore. They expect it in physical education, know why they're doing it, and know it's not a punishment and is meant to help them be the best they can be, and it gets kids up and moving. This culture shift is evident through teacher observation.

This program has been a good advertisement for PE and health, definitely overlooked sometimes in schools. The positive things PE teachers do and the positive impact on overall impact on health are sometimes overlooked in schools. The FitnessBowl devotes specific attention to why health and fitness are important and is a celebration of those kids who aren't necessarily athletic but are willing to take time to be fit.

The FitnessBowl changed the culture of what is expected in health and physical education. Yes, there will be lifelong activities, but also health-related fitness because that's what students are going to use to stay healthy for a lifetime, changing their perspective on health and PE and why it's important. The results from other PE teachers in the district are good as well.

From running the FitnessBowl, Adam has learned how spreading the wealth and helping other people buy in is crucial. Included in this is having a way to pitch a vision and helping people understand it's okay if things aren't exactly perfect in year I. It may not look like the original plan, but together you can get there. If you have a vision in your mind, it just may take a few steps to get there, and that's okay. It's always going to be tough the first time, but each time it definitely gets better, easier, and more efficient. Adam encouraged, "Helping people around you understand that is crucial even if they disagree or don't see it. Believe in yourself. You're going to get there. It might take some time, but you've got to give it a couple of times to really see if it's successful."

Preparation for teacher leadership started in Adam's undergraduate experience. Teacher leadership was talked about and expected. Successful teaching was discussed as more than just teaching a class, and teacher candidates were encouraged to take on roles to create and improve successful programs. South Carolina Alliance for Health, Physical Education, Recreation and Dance (SCAHPERD) provides sessions that teach how to promote and advocate for a program. Physical education doesn't have standardized test scores, so PE teachers must go out of their way to educate the general public on what PE and health programs contribute and how to promote a successful health and PE program.

Strengths Adam sees in his own teacher leadership include contributing to the success of this project through time, productivity, and focus. Adam shared that at this point in his life, just finding and putting time in outside of school hours is difficult, as there are never enough hours in a regular school day. Therefore, one strength is to use time productively. Keep pushing for things you think are important. Never give up, which is difficult because there are definitely boundaries in a school setting that are very difficult to cross. To address these boundaries, think creatively and continuously strive to improve. These are the strengths of teacher leaders.

Some areas for self-improvement Adam identifies as he continues his journey in teacher leadership are delegating and patience. Delegating tasks, having more involvement, being patient, and realizing that you don't have to do everything "right now" are skills Adam recognizes from running this program that he has, but must hone. Adam stated, "It's a process and something I will get better at over time."

When asked how his experiences as a teacher leader have shaped how he thinks about himself as an educator, Adam shared how a lot of his experiences have increased his confidence in the important things he does for the children, school, and community. He's been pushed to make the biggest impact he can for the children. He's been fortunate to be around some really good PE teachers who are also good leaders and have greatly influenced him.

Teacher leadership has made Adam a better person in working with people who are different than himself and have different perspectives, and have made him an overall stronger individual. He acknowledged the hard work of teachers and how teacher leaders take on additional duties beyond regular teaching duties. A great benefit of teacher leadership is the impact one has on one's students, community, colleagues, and school.

In 2018, Adam was working on his doctorate (PhD) in health education and promotion. Though he loved working in the classroom, a tough realization settled in him in that he might have a bigger impact on a larger community setting in PE or health if he left his classroom. His short-term goal for two to three years was to be the absolute best teacher he could be and complete his PhD program. Moving beyond that time frame, he identified some possibilities: leading a nonprofit related to health and trying to make the biggest impact he can as far as wellness goes or becoming more involved with an organization like SCAHPERD in a higher leadership position.

Adam recognizes the leaders he's been around are much more experienced and knowledgeable. He also acknowledges it's fun to be involved with people who are way better at what they do so others can learn and grow. Therefore, his five-year plan is to grow to be a stronger leader, a more patient leader, better at delegating and more productive. Working with people who view things differently, have different perspectives and different personalities can be a challenge. Learning how to work with people toward a common goal is something he hopes to improve on, see he's getting better at, and demonstrate how he's learned to work with all kinds of people.

A final thought from Adam is that people who are working with teachers need to understand that they can't be so humble. Teachers are humble, wonderful, and hardworking, but they need to advocate and promote what they're doing, because people need to know! The amazing number of hours they invest and how much they care about their students cannot be kept silent. Everybody needs to know what a wonderful job you're doing to promote education and not necessarily yourself, regardless of the area you work in. More teachers and teacher preparation programs need to learn to do this.

PEARL STANTON, SPEECH PATHOLOGIST AND COMMUNITY ADVOCATE, CENTRAL WISCONSIN

Another path for teacher leaders is through advocacy and policy. Pearl Stanton's (a pseudonym) teacher leader path is powered in two ways: first, by the advocacy role she plays as a speech pathologist, and second, by the opportunity she had to learn about and engage in policy and advocacy initiatives as a member and officer in a teachers' union in Wisconsin.

Pearl is a speech and language pathologist who works in a public school district in Wisconsin. For more than ten years she's worked in a grade school serving students in kindergarten through sixth grade, and in 2018 had a caseload of 47 students.

In Pearl's school there are 600 students, and while diversity is limited, the student body includes a large Hmong population, some Hispanic students, and still fewer African American students. Demographics show 75% are Caucasian and 25% are minorities; 75% of her students are male and 25% are female. Pearl's school includes families who live on farms in the country, as well as those who live in suburban apartments and affluent estates. About 27% of the families she serves are eligible for free and reduced lunches.

Pearl describes the district she serves as urban and the sixth largest district in a state with 435 school districts. The district encompasses families from six communities and serves just under 100,000 students. There are 16 elementary schools, 3 middle schools, and 3 high schools in the district. Wisconsin has a voucher system that allows families at charter and parochial schools to obtain services like speech. While speech therapists in Pearl's district are assigned to charter and parochial schools where students receive about 50% of the services they would receive in a public school setting, she does not serve in this capacity.

Through over 31 years of work with students, Pearl has learned to look carefully at data, but also to look at the context of the data, such as where and how children live. She has learned not to make assumptions based on the comfort of one's own skin. With regard to teacher leadership, Pearl notes that her school district is fairly good at involving teachers in the decision-making process or shared leadership. She explains that teachers are involved in all committees and initiatives under way in the district. The district leadership team includes a superintendent and four assistant superintendents who each support a different aspect of teaching and learning in the district.

At the building level, Pearl describes her principal as a good collaborator. Every day is a collaborative effort. Some teachers want to be a part of that process and some don't, and teachers can opt in or out of leadership responsibilities. Core to the drive in opportunity for teachers has been a school improvement grant. The grant allows a range of classroom and special education teachers to be involved in the planning process for each school, though in terms of formal (paid) and informal (unpaid) roles, there are far more informal, unpaid roles.

For example, teachers on the positive behavioral interventions and supports (PBIS) committee receive a stipend, but teachers who are asked to serve on the CSIP (continuous school improvement plan) or curriculum committees do not receive any compensation. Pearl has served on a lot of committees, and even when not asked or compensated, she has always felt welcome and even encouraged to advocate, especially for special education kids.

Pearl's initial license was in elementary education, but she continued in graduate school to become a speech pathologist. In addition to her work with students and multiple committees at the school and district levels, she also worked with a variety of student teachers, supervised graduate students in assistive technology, and taught as an adjunct faculty member. Pearl explained that it was always important to her to give back, to be intentional about getting better, and to pay it forward. Pearl states, "My life has been blessed and I have been privileged to live this professional life—this life as a teacher leader." She attributes her enthusiasm for education, resilience, and success to the many people who supported and mentored her, including a remarkable foster family and multiple mentors. Pearl pays it forward through her service to students, student teachers, new teachers, peers, families, her school, district, community, and state.

Pearl has been a member of the teachers' union for over 30 years. She credits her participation in the union as the place where she honed her skills in legislative and political action when she stepped up to fill a legislative liaison position vacated by another member. This opportunity helped her learn about political action and develop voice as well as her passion for civic engagement. It was a passion for equitable education for all that fueled her most recent teacher leader project.

Pearl is a founding member and leader of the Fox Cities Advocates for Public Education, a not-for-profit organization that collaborates with, but operates outside, the public school system. The organization is a public advocacy group that includes parents and families, as well as educators and others who are working to garner support for public education. Core beliefs of the organization include the following: strong public education is vital to preparing children for their future and preserving democracy; public money should be used for public schools; and local control must be preserved so that taxpayer-funded schools are accountable to the public.

As a nonpartisan organization, Fox Cities Advocates for Public Education does not support or oppose candidates for public office. It takes positions on issues, but not political parties. That is not to say, however, that Pearl does not talk with legislators and lobbyists to help them make informed decisions—she does! In addition, she works with the group to establish community events that provide information and a forum for discussion of critical legislation and opportunities to impact public opinion.

Pearl's advocacy group produces voting guides and plans informative events around school funding, elections, school vouchers, and current legislation. Many of these issues are complex, so Pearl and the organization provide a service to the public by breaking down the information and presenting it in easily consumable chunks. Ultimately, the organization works to provide the best possible education for all children through education of all adults.

Pearl explains that leadership is nothing she specialized in during college, but that she sees how important it is to advocate for children and to step up. "Everyone is busy, but it could be your voice that makes a difference for someone else." She believes it's one's civic duty to share what one knows, which she does even when others don't agree. Pearl would say, "That's okay. I just agree to disagree. That's democracy!"

Asked where she thought she'd be in five years, she says, "I will always be active and involved, and education will always have my heart. Honestly, I will be doing anything that will help someone else." For Pearl that's what teacher leaders do: they serve and help others by developing, finding, and sharing resources; providing information; distributing guidelines; and assisting others in gaining access and opportunities. They provide a foundation or a framework for others to build on. Pearl says of herself, "Anyone can do what I have done and maybe even better—I hope better!"

CHARLOTTE BRENNER, LEARNING SUPPORT TEACHER, ROYAL HEIGHTS ELEMENTARY, SURREY, BRITISH COLUMBIA

One way to support change in schools is through facilitation of professional development that promotes authentic forms of collaboration, engagement, and ownership among teachers. This case study describes a three-year professional development (PD) project in which educators worked together to connect self-regulated learning (SRL) to an inquiry-based curriculum. The case study illustrates the contextual pressures on and opportunities for developing meaningful and teacher-led PD.

The case centers on Charlotte Brenner's role as a learning support teacher and PD chair. Charlotte served as a point person to support her colleagues during a period when significant changes were happening at multiple levels (i.e., classroom, school, neighborhood, district, and provincial). While Charlotte abstains from the label of *leader*, being a facilitator of change is central to her identity as a teacher:

> I am passionate about moving things forward. It has happened throughout my career. It was something I tried to do when I initially entered teaching and it was something that you had to do. You really had to fight for it. I encountered a lot of back talk about it. I see myself really as more of a coordinator than a leader because I am part of the staff. I like to guide things along.

Although Charlotte does not use *leadership* in describing her role in this project, one of her allies in this project, Dr. Nancy Perry, explains, "Charlotte and the principal, Catherine, have worked closely to support this transformation, but none of it would have happened without Charlotte's leadership."

Teachers often find themselves experiencing constant waves of change from a variety of sources. While change is expected in education, it poses simultaneous opportunities and threats when moving new ideas forward. An important element in how successfully educational changes are advanced is the school context. Who are the students, teachers, and leaders? What resources are available? Where and when are the changes being implemented? What is the school culture within which the changes are expected?

Surrey School District is the largest public school district in British Columbia, serving the cities of Surrey and White Rock as well as Barnston Island. Royal Heights Elementary is located in Surrey, a city of over 500,000 residents located near Vancouver, and enrolls approximately 200 students in grades K–7. More than half of Royal Heights' students are English learners, including a relatively large number from Punjabi, as well as Vietnamese and Chinese, Syrian refugee, and Aboriginal students. The students learn together in multiage classrooms, sometimes spanning as many as three grade levels, but primarily organized as split-grade-level classrooms.

Charlotte is Royal Heights' learning support teacher, having taught in urban schools her entire 22-year career with teaching qualifications as an early childhood educator and special educator. As a learning support teacher, Charlotte has varied responsibilities that integrate the roles of special educator, instructional coach, reading specialist, professional development coordinator, and co-teacher. Part of her responsibilities involve supporting teachers as they implement new practices and organizing professional development at the school. A daily component of her role is working with students, typically students who have experienced difficulties in learning to read and students who do not speak English. Some of her support is based in the classroom, while the other half involves working with students outside their classrooms. Most of the students do not have designations for special education services, and Charlotte feels she is given a lot of latitude in how she structures support for student and teacher learning.

Given her role, Charlotte was uniquely positioned when a series of changes impacted Royal Heights Elementary. The Surrey District had designated Royal Heights Elementary as a choice school with two curriculum tracks (i.e., a school within a school). The Discovery Program, an inquiry-based and one of six district-wide choice programs, was moved to the school and offered in parallel to the more traditional curriculum. The introduction of the Discovery Program began amid changes in principals, faculty, and curricula, which impacted school culture. In addition to the inquiry-based curricula, there was a district- and school-level focus on SRL, and Royal Heights welcomed a new principal who was dedicated to promoting SRL. But some teachers were more comfortable with the traditional curriculum, and SRL was not yet well understood.

As new pro-SRL, inquiry-based faculty were hired, tensions arose among the faculty and some teachers chose to leave the school. A few teachers openly resisted the changes; for example, commenting that the new curriculum represented the *flavor of the day* and labeling the students in the choice program the *discovery kids*. This discord resulted in staff turnover of both veteran and new teachers. Additionally, there was community resistance when some families expressed their preference for the more traditional school curriculum. At the same time, British Columbia changed its provincial curriculum from one that was traditional with prescribed learning outcomes to a competency-based model, adding new curricular pressures.

What might have seemed like the vortex of too much change became a nexus of opportunity through Charlotte's facilitation. The principal in the school at the time worked with Charlotte to transform the Discovery Program and rebrand it. This rebranding involved integrating SRL practices to support the inquiry learning program. When Catherine, a new principal, joined the school, she worked with staff to connect these inquiries with areas of teacher interest such as studying First Peoples, environmental issues, and integrating social emotional learning (SEL). Charlotte's ideas for integration and transformation resonated with a small group of Discovery Program teachers, and a series of voluntary after-school PD sessions began.

No formal plan was created to support teachers' professional development in SRL. Rather, Charlotte's ideas for PD in SRL obtained support from collaborators as needed. While the PD opportunities may have seemed serendipitous, Charlotte was in a unique position to connect people and share possibilities, driven by her passion to move ideas forward. Three groups of allies were critical. First, Charlotte had the support of Royal Heights' principal, who was hired to promote SRL and served as an advocate for the school. Therefore, the shift to focus on SRL was being supported at district and school levels, which made it possible for the principal to actively support and seek out new faculty who wanted to promote SRL in meaningful ways.

With the Discovery Program and new pro-SRL faculty, the second group of allies was the teachers who wanted to learn how to improve SRL in their classrooms. Third, Charlotte also had the support of her professor at the University of British Columbia (UBC), Dr. Nancy Perry, an educational psychologist whose scholarship focused on SRL in elementary schools. So rather than starting a new PD initiative and adding on to what teachers already had to do, Charlotte conceptualized the SRL PD as a way to transform the Discovery Program and integrate the curriculum. Nancy volunteered to support interested faculty in learning about SRL, and Charlotte organized a few voluntary sessions after school.

The informal meetings were scheduled every month or so throughout the year and evolved into two-hour collaboration sessions during which teachers shared their progress with Charlotte's and Nancy's support. These sessions, which are known as the SRL Learning Team Meetings, began with a few teachers. Then some serving as temporary teachers at Royal Heights wanted to stay connected after they were reassigned to other schools, and they returned for sessions. Doctoral students from UBC visited sessions to learn more about how the teachers apply SRL in their classrooms. Charlotte describes the SRL Team meetings as being very fluid, with different people joining the regular group of Royal Heights faculty a few times a year. Over time as more teachers adopted SRL strategies, the entire Royal Heights faculty began attending the sessions.

The SRL Team Meetings evolved over a three-year period, becoming more teacher-led and collaborative. Teachers develop individual SRL goals for their classrooms. Typically they select a specific focus student and then use this as their learning case, from which they generalize instructional strategies for other students. Teachers also identify a content area or topic and often work together outside the sessions with other interested teachers. For example, these topic areas have involved integrating SRL strategies in curricula on indigenous people, environmental and place-based learning, and student mental health and well-being.

In the first year of the SRL Team Meetings, the initial three meetings were organized to bring in Nancy's expertise about SRL. The meetings provided a shared understanding of SRL and connected concepts to what teachers were already doing in their classrooms. As Charlotte explains, "We had a different superintendent and different ideas about what SRL looked like in the classroom. Nancy's approach was quite different than what the District was funneling down. So she did that very carefully." After these initial conversations with the teachers, Nancy and Charlotte discussed the teachers' requests for more support, and Charlotte provided follow-up.

For example, Charlotte co-taught a poetry unit with a new teacher in a multiage Discovery Program class who had requested more guidance. The two teachers designed the poetry unit around providing the fifth-, sixth-, and seventh-grade students with more choice in activities and assessment, aligning the unit with Nancy's key strategies. Working with differentiated resources, the students selected four or five forms of poetry and worked in small groups to learn about the different poetry forms. All the elements of the SRL framework were integrated: mini lessons to support strategy development, choice, appropriate challenge, collaboration, teacher/peer support, and opportunities to monitor progress and make changes in light of ongoing feedback. The class also created their own criteria for self-assessment of their poetry portfolios.

In the second and third years of SRL Team Meetings, only an initial session was needed to review SRL concepts to build a shared understanding. Also, the participating teachers began to set the meeting agenda. Important norms developed within the sessions, which supported their success. First, all the teachers chose their own strategies, tools, or resources. For example, the SRL framework chosen for the poetry unit was not the only conceptual framework the teachers discussed. Other approaches, such as zones of regulation, were adopted for integrating SRL.

In addition, all teachers shared ideas on self-assessment in daily classroom activities and in more formal digital portfolios to explore applications of SRL. And finally, the teachers began to share their mistakes in the meetings, demonstrating a strong sense of community and trust, which Charlotte labeled as being truthful with each other. As for Charlotte's role, that too evolved, and she moved from coordinator to team member: "I like to share what I'm doing, but we have a very high functioning staff so I'm a piece of that puzzle."

Several contextual factors positively influenced the development of SRL Team Meetings. First, Charlotte describes a new openness to SRL by multiple stakeholders. The district publicized the importance of SRL, the new British Columbia curriculum focused on SRL, and Nancy made herself available to provide the opportunity to learn about SRL, as needed. Meeting participants were ready to learn about SRL. Royal Heights faculty was open to considering different ways of teaching, and Nancy was open to looking at other ways to approach SRL, such as through environmental studies and student mental health. Second, there was a sense of freedom that welcomed everyone's ideas and provided flexibility in professional development. As Charlotte describes, "[Teachers] really did feel they could do their own thing. It was not just words."

A third important factor was that Charlotte had allies in school administration, in the school, and at the district level for the SRL Team Meetings. During the three-year process there were two new principals at Royal Heights. Charlotte describes how each principal brought the needed skill set at the right time. When the school needed changes, the principal was a positive and fearless advocate for SRL. The current school principal, who is very adept at facilitating relationships, helps to sustain and build on progress.

In addition, the Surrey School District has been supportive by promoting the SRL program development at Royal Heights. And the school board has been supportive, initially being drawn to the school because of the Discovery Program being relocated there, but then becoming aware of the SRL framework being used. In fact, one board member has been very supportive by attending multiple meetings with the community to help parents understand the value of the SRL focus.

Success of the SRL Team Meetings can be evidenced in multiple ways. As described previously, teachers are actively involved in meetings and set the agenda. For example, Charlotte says that at the final meeting at the end of year three, she and Nancy turned to each other and shared that they had said very little during the meeting, and that's where they wanted to get to. Moreover, the SRL Team Meetings are part of a larger process for teacher-led PD. For their formal PD, the teachers select topics four or five times a year.

Charlotte explains that before the SRL Team Meetings involved the entire faculty, everyone would choose different individual activities, but now they plan their PD days together. For example, for one of the PD days scheduled in the summer at the end of the third year of SRL Team Meetings, all the teachers decided on an environmental focus that integrated SRL. They designed a

PD day with an environmental educator coming in to speak and then planned time to collaborate and make the connections to SRL. As Charlotte describes, this collaborative, teacher-led PD shows signs of expanding. "People are already wanting to start working for October planning. They want a First Peoples focus and how the First Peoples ways of knowing promote SRL."

The hallmark of successful PD is student outcomes, and Charlotte can see multiple ways in which the teacher-led SRL PD efforts have been impactful for Royal Heights' students. Although it is optional within the district, all the Royal Heights teachers have adopted a digital portfolio platform that provides students, families, and teachers with ongoing formative and summative assessments. The digital portfolios archive student artifacts across the school years. Students continuously examine their progress and set goals, which families also can view and comment on. Charlotte notes that in her work with students, she observes their engagement in SRL and consistently hears them use the language that reflects teachers' knowledge and application of SRL. Charlotte also hears her colleagues discuss their knowledge of each other's classrooms.

The Royal Heights school culture has transformed into one where all teachers create time for sharing ideas with each other. However, Charlotte acknowledges that there are still areas for growth and that teachers often discuss that they are not quite there. Teachers benefit from talking about ideas, but they want more in-time support in their classrooms.

Charlotte would like to see the SRL Team Meetings expanded to other schools in the district. She sees herself refocusing on the teachers and what she can do to support them, recognizing how her work with colleagues supports their students. She is also more focused on how to get other people involved to support the faculty's interests. Charlotte also views herself as having grown through this process. "I'm much more open to vetting others' ideas. [I'm] starting to understand that implementation is always changing, and the wealth of knowledge that others bring to the conversation. I'm not so stuck on what people bring to the table and what can be made from that."

Charlotte sees this case study as sharing how to successfully promote teacher engagement in professional development. She believes it is essential to consider the contextual influences that are needed for teachers to engage, feel successful, and take ownership of their professional learning. In 2018, Charlotte began exploring how supporting teachers' competence, autonomy, and relatedness is important to their professional growth and fits well with SRL. Charlotte finds herself in the perfect role for facilitating this growth, as she describes in concluding an interview for this case study. "I'm in a sweet position—I can see it all."

SUMMARY

This chapter examined observable behaviors through which teacher leaders in specialist, noncore positions provide coaching, mentoring, advocacy, and the opportunity to have an impact at the district level, state level, or beyond. The case studies in this chapter are anchored in a model that promotes professional learning and growth. The teacher leaders highlighted in this chapter exemplified how one develops a collaborative culture that creates and supports organizational change and works with stakeholders to ensure learner growth and advancement of the profession.

Additionally, the teacher leaders highlighted accurately anticipated the needs of each learner and proactively implement strategies to improve student learning; advocate for instruction that supports the needs of all learners; and use multiple strategies to harness the skills, expertise, and knowledge of colleagues to address curricular expectations and student learning needs (Strike, Fitzsimmons, & Hornberger, 2019).

Research clearly indicates the impact of leadership on student achievement (Marzano, Waters, & McNulty, 2005; Reeves, 2006). Using leadership data helps determine the quality and consistency of leadership practices and adds insight into which leadership practices are most effective in building capacity, creating culture, and sustaining student achievement (White, 2007).

REFLECTIVE QUESTIONS AND APPLICATION

1. Reflect on the leadership of each teacher highlighted in this chapter. Place him/her on the rubric provided in the figures near the beginning of the chapter and justify your placement.
2. Ten powerful acts of leadership are to modify time, modify opportunities, provide corrective feedback, replicate successful practices, make midcourse corrections, analyze diverse types of data, collaboratively implement and evaluate common assessments, develop and test hypotheses, tailor training to needs, and commit resources (White, 2007). Compare this list to the case studies featured in this chapter and determine which acts of leadership are represented.
3. Self-assessment: reflecting on your own experiences and actions, place yourself on the rubrics provided in the figures near the beginning of this chapter. What area(s) of strength stand out, and what might you do to improve or obtain additional experience?
4. Identify the vision and purpose of the work of each teacher leader.

5. What were some of the challenges in translating each teacher leader's vision into operational terms? What alternatives or changes might you recommend? Is this something you have, or something that could work in your own setting? If not, what changes would need to be made for it to work in your own setting?
6. What contributes to each leader's success?
7. What aspects of each story resonated with you, and what did you learn from each story that might help in your own practice?
8. What observations have you made in looking at the leadership highlighted in this chapter, specific to teacher leadership at the specialist level, compared to that shared in other chapters? Would you say teacher leadership is easier to plan and implement within the specialist setting? Why or why not?

REFERENCES

Cooper Institute. (2018). *Fitness Gram components*. Retrieved from http://www.cooperinstitute.org/fitnessgram/components

Marzano, R. J., Waters, T., & McNulty, B. A. (2005). *School leadership that works: From research to results*. Alexandria, VA: Association for Supervision and Curriculum Development.

Reeves, D. B. (2006). *The learning leader: How to focus school improvement for better results*. Alexandria, VA: Association for Supervision and Curriculum Development.

Strike, K., Fitzsimmons, J., & Hornberger, R. (2019). *Identifying and growing internal leaders: A framework for effective teacher leadership*. Lanham, MD: Rowman & Littlefield.

Surrey Schools. (2017). *Leadership in learning*. Retrieved from https://surreylearning bydesign.ca/school-plans/royalheights/royal-heights-elementary-2/

White, S. (2007). Data on purpose: Due diligence to increase student achievement. In D. Reeves (Ed.), *Ahead of the curve: The power of assessment to transform teaching and learning*. Bloomington, IN: Solution Tree Press.

Chapter Seven

Teacher Leader on Special Assignment (TOSA)

This chapter focuses on teacher leaders who are engaged in special assignments. The assignment may be one of the teacher leader's own choosing, as in the case of Meghan Everette; one of an organization's choosing, as we find in Tina's situation; or perhaps a blended assignment that is derived in part by the teacher leader and in part by one or more stakeholders, such as in Teri's case.

As we consider the four cases in this chapter, we invite you to use a bifocal lens that focuses on the teacher leaders' ability to engage all stakeholders, as well as more advanced advocacy skills. Being able to engage all of one's stakeholders is a critical competency that is a foundation for building other more advanced teacher leader skills and effecting change in a community. In order to be effective, teacher leaders must learn to look intentionally at *all* of the stakeholders in their community, even those that are disenfranchised. Teacher leaders have to ask how they can engage each and every stakeholder in a singular effort.

Case studies in this chapter reflect many domains in the Framework for Effective Teacher Leadership (Strike, Fitzsimmons, & Hornberger, 2019). However, as you read each of these cases studies, consider elements from Critical Competencies "1b: Engages all stakeholders" and the element "Builds community through a concerted, collaborative effort to reach out to disenfranchised or disengaged populations" (see figure 7.1) and Advocacy "4a: Practices and refines resourcefulness" and the element "Advocates for resources financial, human, material, professional development, training, and time to meet the needs of all learners" (see figure 7.2).

Specifically, examine the four cases that follow in terms of the way(s) each teacher leader considers the stakeholders in the community and reaches out to

1b: Engages all stakeholders.	Level of Performance			
Element	Ineffective	Initiating	Developing	Effective
Builds community through a concerted collaborative effort to reach out to disenfranchised or disengaged populations	Misses or declines the opportunity to reach disenfranchised or disengaged populations and build a community.	Values community and begins to use some strategies to connect with some populations on a limited basis.	Collaborates and builds community with some populations regularly.	Connects with all populations to build community.

Figure 7.1. Partial rubric for Framework for Effective Teacher Leadership (1b).
Copyright © Strike, Fitzsimmons, & Hornberger, 2019.

4a. Practices and refines resourcefulness	Level of Performance			
Element	Ineffective	Initiating	Developing	Effective
Advocates for resources (financial, human, material, professional development, training and time) to meet the needs of all learners.	Fails to advocate for resources (financial, human, material, professional development, training and time) to meet the needs of all learners.	Attempts to advocate for resources (financial, human, material, professional development, training and time) to meet the needs of all learners.	Actively advocates for resources (financial, human, material, professional development, training and time) to meet the needs of all learners.	Develops a collaborative culture that advocates for resources (financial, human, material, professional development, training and time) to meet the needs of all learners.

Figure 7.2. Partial rubric for Framework for Effective Teacher Leadership (4a).
Copyright © Strike, Fitzsimmons, & Hornberger, 2019.

engage each group in collective action. Note how each handles challenging attitudes ands builds and engages the community. Teacher leaders must put themselves *out there* to learn and understand the populations who make up their communities in order to solve problems together. It is often not easy, and sometimes the result isn't exactly as the teacher leader hoped, but the community, nevertheless, is engaged, and that is important long term.

Consider advocacy. Advocacy is a more advanced teacher leader skill. It requires not only knowledge of resources, but also skill in implementing that knowledge to effect change. Note how teacher leaders spotlighted here garner public support for changing assessment measures and procedures, as in Jodie's work, or find equitable solutions for diverse students across a broad spectrum of school communities, like in Tina's case. Note how the teacher leaders gather the resources—financial, human, and material—necessary to make instructional, procedural, or policy changes that they know will advantage *all* students in a school or district, as Meghan does in her case. As you study these cases, consider ways you would garner support for a change that you knew would chart a more productive course for your fellow teachers or for the students in your district.

JODIE JANTZ, MIDDLE SCHOOL TEACHER AND TEST COORDINATOR, GOODRICH MIDDLE SCHOOL, LINCOLN, NEBRASKA

The purpose of this case study was to streamline standardized testing practices. The district has used standardized tests for over 15 years. At the state level, Nebraska is now in the adaptive assessment phase, where some standardized assessments reflect benchmark formative assessment with data that can be used the next day. As the test coordinator, Jodie works with staff in multiple ways throughout this project, creating a testing schedule, sharing instructional strategies, and training staff on how to effectively use technology and how to get around the glitches that arise with any computer-based project. She provides training on how to give a standardized assessment, providing accommodations and ensuring that students receive the appropriate accommodations.

Goodrich Middle School is a suburban school located in Lincoln, Nebraska, that serves students in grades 6 through 8. As the second largest school district in the state, the district has thirty-nine public elementary, twelve public middle, and six public high schools, along with nine focus schools, including the new Career Academy, allowing high school students to receive dual credit with a local community college. There are over 41,000 students and 6,442 contracted employees in the district. Goodrich Middle School has 78 teachers. Approximately 47% of students are white, 11% are African American, 6% are Asian, 26% are Hispanic, and 8% are multiracial, with the remainder falling under Native American and Native Pacific.

Goodrich is a well-maintained, 50-year-old building in a suburban location. There are approximately 866 students, of whom 76% qualify for free and reduced lunch. Of the population, 13% are English Language Learners

(ELL), with the largest community speaking Arabic and Kurdish, closely followed by Spanish. The school also has 20% of students identified as special education and 8% as gifted and talented. The school serves as a pilot school for reading and mathematics intervention, requiring an additional 30 minutes on a reading goal and a math goal each day for all students. Goodrich is also implementing innovative design thinking within many classrooms, and students can take classes in coding, Chinese, and robotics.

The district prides itself on the collective self-efficacy practices of John Hattie, which hold that all teachers can be leaders, and incorporates the Danielson Framework for teaching and leadership. This is piggybacking on the idea that all administrators should be bringing teachers up through the ranks as leaders. Over the past 10 years, the district has implemented a very specific way of moving staff into administration. An administrator recommends the teacher be part of an administration cohort led by the district office. Once participants successfully completed this district-level training, they can then be interviewed for coordinator positions (SPED, student services, instructional coordinator). To qualify for the administration cohort, the person must have at least three years of teaching experience. Most administrators have 5–10 years before moving into a coordinator position.

At the building level these positions and duties are often divided differently, and often teachers assume some of the responsibilities. Coordinators are teachers who receive additional pay (i.e., as test coordinator Jodie receives an extra $5,408 per year). Some of the responsibilities filter down through teachers, but it's a back-and-forth model, and principals have the authority and flexibility to make changes.

There were four intended outcomes for this case study, and they are fundamental. The first was that every student would be tested. There is high mobility in the district, and while completion of testing was between 94 and 95%, the goal was 100%.

The second outcome was to set up a system that streamlined testing, provided a comfortable environment, reduced anxiety, and built relationships between teachers and students. The third outcome was for everyone who needed accommodations to demonstrate their knowledge to receive it. Whether a student needs to stand and stretch or wear a headset, students' needs must be known and addressed. When students are comfortable, they can give 100% and do their best, which in turn allows for the data to be as valid as possible. Finally, teachers must be comfortable. Teachers need to know that they will not be compared against each other based on the results of the test scores of their students and within the district, and Nebraska teachers' evaluations are not based on student test scores. Teachers must be encouraged to utilize the data.

As an educator, Jodie has a noted love-hate relationship with assessment. On the one hand, formative assessment is used on a daily basis to help guide instruction. On the other hand, many times an exam is given and the purpose is unclear. There are aspects of our hyper-focus on testing that have been good, such as examining instruction and relooking at professional learning opportunities. New teachers come better prepared, and veteran teachers are better utilizing available data.

In 2016, Jodie accepted the position of test coordinator within her school, managing all tests given by district or state so they could be taken efficiently, allowing teachers and students to focus on learning. There were four teachers district-wide serving in this capacity, as test coordinators. Jodie was asked to do this because she is a data person, and organization is in her skill set. She must think outside the box and collaborate with all staff to get schedules just right.

At that time testing throughout the school was semi-computer-based and had moved to 100% computer-based. During Jodie's first year, all SPED students used paper and pencil to test, which required coordination of 260 to 290 paper-pencil tests as each student took two or three different tests. Students had test booklets and a teacher to read the tests to them. The following year SPED students were allowed to have the math test read to them, but not the reading test; the year after that, students were not allowed to have any of the tests read to them, and all accommodations for having a test read were made through the use of a text-to-speech feature on their computers.

In 2017, the district purchased a new testing system through Northwest Evaluation Association (NWEA) through a deal in which the district also acquired the Measures of Academic Progress (MAP). In 2018, the MAP was piloted at the seventh-grade level, and in the following year the entire school took the MAP test two times unless the student was in a reading class, and then he/she took the reading portion three times. Jodie trained 50 teachers on how to administer the MAP, which is viewed as a useful tool with data available the next day. Jodie ensured that the test was administered as efficiently as possible, then her role changed to more of a technical one, such as ensuring accurate class lists, accommodations, and user-friendly options for the teacher.

Jodie also works closely with her administrator to ensure schedules are coordinated, planning time is received, and data are analyzed to make instructional adjustments.

Jodie works with teachers individually to address specific issues or needs such as their comfort level using technology; mentor; modify curriculum; access resources; align instructional strategies; and lead the science PLC group. Nebraska does not use test scores for teacher assessment, yet schools are ranked, and results are published in local newspapers. Jodie and others work together to present this information in a more positive light and assist teachers in seeing the benefit of giving a MAP test, which provides specific data about what a student is ready to learn next. This shift in data available to teachers from a standardized test, from data about last year's students to data they can use tomorrow, benefits all students by allowing staff to better accommodate the variety of learners that occurs in every classroom.

Jodie is also working to move teacher thinking from a focus on how many days are dedicated to testing to specific ways to utilize the data provided by the tests. District-level MAP training within their PLC groups has assisted with use and enthusiasm. Jodie shared, "I think it's going to be a good thing for the district if we stay with it, but as many big districts go."

In the past, students needing accommodation were pulled from the general education classrooms for testing. Setting up accommodations can be challenging, as middle school students are often hypersensitive to what others think of them and loath standing out or being different. Jodie works with regular education teachers to encourage students to use the accommodations on a daily basis so that testing accommodations are a continuation and not a change.

For example, Jodie encourages using the text-to-speech feature on their computers for students who struggle in reading or are identified as ELL. During testing, the seating chart has students needing accommodation in the rear of the classroom behind their classmates to encourage use of accommodations while remaining unseen by their peers. One of the most critical aspects of teaching is the relationship that teachers and students develop. Allowing the student to test with his or her regular teacher provides the teacher the opportunity to work with the student with whom that teacher has a relationship.

Testing has been a shift for the SPED teachers on staff. In the past, teachers actively read the test to students. Now they can encourage them, but that's it. There is a push to have four to five students in a group, but if the teacher is not allowed to assist, then there is no reason to have a small number to test, and they can have a group of 10. It will take Jodie a couple of years to work with teachers toward the district declaration that a group of 10 special ed students with headsets on is perfectly acceptable. One of the challenges has been the frustration of feeling that teachers are not supporting students in the manner they think is best. Jodie understands teachers just have to experience the change, and they will move toward the new norm. As more data are reflected upon, adjustments are made at the school, district, and state levels to continue to ensure that all students are being allowed to demonstrate what they know.

Specific to interventions, the 10 teachers who piloted MAP in seventh grade have received a one-hour training and looked at that data. The instructional coaches and administration are responsible, but Jodie anticipates she will have a role in the training and use of MAP data.

Other content areas and specialist areas, such as social studies, science, art, and business, aren't giving the tests or using the data. Jodie anticipates that these teachers who now have access to the data will start to look at them. She hopes to be able to help them use the data to better support students within their classrooms. The use of MAP data as formative assessment can serve to inform cross-curriculum lessons and more fully support student growth.

There was no action plan to guide the process. Jodie had general ideas of end goals, and the actions were modified based on need. One coordinator served as a wonderful mentor specifically on how to have a tough conversation but allow people to walk away feeling good about themselves. Another challenge is the stigma of testing. Teachers are busy, and they all have their own thing going on. They don't want to lose days to testing or anything not tied directly to their curriculum. They aren't thrilled, but it's the very idea of testing that they're not thrilled about. The possibility of having useful data the next day has many teachers very interested, since this hasn't always been the case.

In prior years there was an IOWA test in the fall, and a state test is given to every child in the spring, and the ELL population also had the English Language Proficiency Assessment (ELPA) in the spring. Now with the addition of the MAP test, which can be thought of as a benchmark, the ELL students are hit hard. After the first year, there's hope to make some adjustments to the number of the assessments. If teachers see the benefits, if they can see a better way to gain information about what a student is ready to learn, then they won't be as upset about giving up those days.

As with all assessments given to students, it is essential to understand that how a test is administered, what data are available, who looks at the data, and how the data are used to move students forward all impact day-to-day classrooms. Both students and teachers feel this impact. Jodie recognizes there's a delicate balance so as not to overload people but still help them see what is available.

Collaboration is the key to any school system, and it is exemplified by the principal who worked hard to see that teachers had the time to do just that. She was an endless resource and always available to assist and support Jodie as she took on the test coordinator role. The assistant principal was the test coordinator before taking her current position. She was also an excellent resource, providing advice, and both administrators provided collegiate and physical support when Jodie simply couldn't be in two places at once.

One of the big takeaways for Jodie reinforced the importance of collaboration even at the administrative level. The willingness to jump in and do what needs to be done because it is what students and staff need is why students who struggle grow. Everyone within the school is there because they want students to succeed.

There is also strong district support for staff at all levels to focus on student learning. There are district staff who always listen, are patient, and are helpful with change, understanding that for some change is natural and for others it is more difficult. For example, when two weeks were given for winter testing, the concern was brought forth to the district-level assessment team. A third week was provided before winter break. This allowed testing to be spread out so that learning could still continue in every class.

In addition to administrators and coordinators, the SPED teachers end up taking the brunt of any type of accommodation needs. The ELL teachers bear the burden of any kind of accommodation and just say, "We'll take care of them." All groups are excellent examples of teachers who do what they need to so that students can succeed. Jodie organizes, and they take care of their students. Collaborating with others includes ensuring accommodations are up-to-date or sharing information such as predictive IEP referrals. There is a willingness to be flexible and to communicate back and forth, for example, about what's coming or what's needed. A plan is organized with those who know the needs and know their schedules are equitable and good for the kids. That's one of the perks of collaborating with a staff who genuinely care about their students.

Some unexpected aspects of serving as test coordinator are self-presentation, response to staff, strategies of how to interact with different personalities, and being cognizant of what is said and how so as not to turn the teacher off to testing. These skills are essential for moving from the classroom to working with teachers building-wide. Through observation of administration, the skill to relate to everybody and work with teachers positively has been modeled, and this is an area in which Jodie has experienced self-growth.

District-wide, administrators work with teacher leaders in different ways. Some allow the teacher to lead, while others want to lead and have the teacher leader support them. The district provides the administrator cohort for teacher leaders who have expressed the desire to move into administration. This allows teachers to gain an understanding of how the system works. Once people move into administration, there's another cohort experience that supports them as they grow as administrators.

Set to complete her doctorate, Jodie's personal/professional goal is to be published four times in two years in a professional journal. To further assist staff and students, she aspires to move into a position such as STEM (science, technology, engineering, and math) coordinator or higher education.

Jodie is aware of her skill set and wants to be sure when she moves into a different role that the path is right for her. This awareness comes through personal reflection, educational experience, and conversations with the various administrators who are generous with their time and feedback. Jodie views this willingness to support, assist, and build capacity as one of the most important things an administrator can do for his/her staff. No one goes into education to do a bad job.

TINA NELSON, MIDDLE SCHOOL MATH SPECIALIST, SUBURBAN ILLINOIS

This is a case study of middle school mathematics specialist Tina Nelson (a pseudonym), who also team teaches in a sixth-grade mathematics classroom while wearing a number of leadership hats. Tina's case highlights the fluid and hybrid nature of many teacher leader roles in schools. It also explores the collaborative planning and multitasking skills necessary to work with a variety of stakeholders and students whenever needed.

Tina's K–8 school district serves approximately 1,400 students in three schools: two K–5 elementary schools and one grades 6–8 middle school. She has served in this district for 21 years. Tina is licensed in mathematics, social studies, science, language arts, and teacher leadership. For the first 15 years, Tina was a classroom teacher in sixth- and eighth-grade classrooms, where she taught mathematics, science, and language arts.

In her sixteenth year with the district, Tina transitioned into a math specialist position at the middle school, which was a new position at that time. Initially Tina's position as math specialist involved working mostly as an interventionist and coaching teachers. More recently, her position evolved to include both ends of the Response to Intervention (RtI) Diamond (Ranch View Middle School, 2018).

Throughout the majority of the day, Tina works one on one with students or in small groups. As a math specialist, Tina plans and co-teaches a sixth-grade mathematics class. For this class, she is the mathematics-endorsed teacher in the room. She does the majority of the lesson planning and assessment while sharing the teaching and grading with her teammate.

In addition to being a member of the sixth-grade team, Tina is mathematics department chair across all grade levels (6–8) and the team leader for the "specials." The specials team is comprised of the reading specialists, counselors, and the librarian, who all support students through RtI, social emotional learning, reading, and mathematics.

One school year, as an additional opportunity, Tina found herself coordinating the mathematics acceleration program at the middle school as part of her math specialist responsibilities. This acceleration program was mandated by a state law that took effect in July right before the start of the school year.

Tina had prepared for this mandate by attending a regional office of education conference to gain more information, but initially thought the acceleration program would be coordinated with the gifted program teachers at the middle school.

However, when the two gifted program teachers, Tina, and administrators met over the summer to discuss the pilot of the new sixth-grade mathematics acceleration program prior to implementation, there was no consensus. One teacher decided to move into a core teaching position at the middle school, and the other teacher chose to go on sabbatical, leaving both gifted positions open with an accelerated mathematics sequence yet to be designed.

Going into August, the gifted program positions had not been filled. So Tina began to work with the three mathematics teachers who would help implement the new accelerated mathematics program: a nontenured teacher, a substitute for someone on maternity leave, and a new teacher to the core classroom, formerly in a special education position.

Tina's first thought was to imagine what this reorganization was going to look like on curriculum night when the parents met the mathematics teachers and the new acceleration program was explained. As Tina described, she was looking at this introduction from the perspective of a parent who was expecting a gifted program, and instead mathematics acceleration guidelines were being explained.

Parents' reactions were varied, and Tina addressed them individually just as she was doing with their children's mathematics programs. She recognized that some parents saw placement in a gifted program as a status symbol, and although the new math acceleration provided more equity, there was less certainty. For example, students in the new program would receive acceleration as they pretested out of grade-level material, but they would be closely monitored and return to grade-level work whenever appropriate.

On curriculum night, the eighth-grade parents, who were the most accustomed to the gifted program, gave the most pushback. Parents were not happy that the gifted services were no longer part of the program. Most parents worried about their children not qualifying for the new program, but another concern arose over the possibility of acceleration creating gaps in learning.

The assistant superintendent and principal were consistent supporters for Tina in communicating with the parents. The search process for the gifted program was shared with all the families by both administrators, and they openly expressed their support for the new mathematics acceleration program.

However, it was Tina who had to coordinate the new program. Logistically, she had to monitor all sixth-, seventh-, and eighth-grade students to see if they needed to be accelerated and what additional supports each student needed. She quickly realized that she would not be able to plan for all the RtI sessions for students working below and above grade level by herself.

In the sixth grade an accelerated mathematics class had been formed that was using the seventh-grade text, so Tina worked with four students who needed extra support. In the seventh grade, six students needed extra support and three needed acceleration, which meant they joined the eighth-grade algebra class. And in the eighth grade, four students needed extra support while four needed to be accelerated beyond the algebra class into geometry.

So Tina asked the assistant superintendent for help, and a math coach from one of the elementary schools was assigned to take RtI groups working below grade level two days a week while Tina supported the algebra teacher and pulled out for accelerated students. However, organizing the groups of students for RtI was only a first step. Tina needed to focus on each individual student and monitor the students' mathematics understanding in both their assigned grade level as well as their accelerated classes.

Tina found herself juggling a school schedule that had not yet been synchronized with the new acceleration program. She needed to be available to support the mathematics teachers, especially those who were being challenged with the acceleration for the first time and to help communicate with parents. Tina continued with her support of the 14 students who needed Tier II RtI extra support to meet grade level standards and the 7 students who needed individual acceleration. And she continued to co-teach a sixth-grade mathematics class as well as carrying her other leadership roles and responsibilities.

One of the new challenges that Tina discovered was working with students who qualified for acceleration yet needed individual support. For example, one student who could easily do the advanced mathematics struggled with any writing involved. Another accelerated student needed additional support because there were several unpredicted gaps in her understanding.

Moving forward, Tina could see where she needed to provide leadership. In working with the eighth graders, Tina found that she needed to coordinate with the high school and align the acceleration program with the potential coursework the students would take next year. She also identified where the schedule needed to be changed so that every student who required extra support or acceleration received instruction on a regular basis with the best possible teacher. About the gifted program, Tina stated:

> I definitely think that going forward we will see that as we can roll 6th grade into 7th grade and into the 8th grade, we will have built a program where parents will understand the middle school does it differently than the elementary school. The idea of a gifted program won't be expected.

In an imperfect transition with unexpected twists and turns, Tina viewed moving forward in a very positive and collaborative light:

> I'm very fortunate my math department has always been very supportive of me. I tell them often, "You make me look good and I appreciate what you do." I always let them know that I am there for them, if they need anything from me. And they are very much on track with me, letting me know what unit they are in and what unit they are heading into. There are days when I'm at a loss and I'm not sure what I should be doing with these kids and there are days when they funnel activities to me.

Tina reciprocates the support by saying, "Hey I think everyone would benefit from this—try this out."

Tina enjoys working with both ends of the RtI Diamond but also explained, "I want to focus on the middle too because that is where most students are. I can't lose that focus." Although this case study was being collected midyear during the transition, Tina already could see how the mathematics program would evolve. She expected the second year to look a lot different and be better.

One of the ways Tina wanted to move forward was to better coordinate resources for acceleration in mathematics. When building the program for extra support, she explained that this coordination had been ongoing for five years. Tina looked forward to the process of developing acceleration curriculum and organizing materials, saying, "This keeps me on my toes, and is brand new, so it puts a fire under me." She knew that the full capacity of what was possible would take time but was excited about the possibilities.

Tina explained that implementing schedule changes took time and that she planned to spend the 2018 to 2019 school year working with the principal because she felt that rearranging the schedule would probably affect an entire grade level. However, she emphasized that it was important to address the schedule because it was a critical component in benefiting both students who needed extra support and students who needed acceleration.

Tina acknowledged that scheduling was only part of a solution. From experience, she knew they would need a plan B when logistics didn't work out (e.g., a mathematics teacher or coach was absent). The hardest part of scheduling coordination was matching students who needed support and students who needed acceleration with the appropriate instructional resources and teachers.

The new program was very fluid, and Tina wanted the students to experience it that way. As she explained, she wanted students to understand that they were getting exactly what they needed: "Just because you're out with Ms. Nelson for this unit, it doesn't mean you'll be out next time."

In terms of teacher leadership, Tina described how wearing all the different hats helped her see the big picture, especially the parent hat. It was always clear to Tina with regard to the significance of the accelerated program because at the middle school level it's really important for students to start determining their future and where they're going with it. She wanted students to feel confident and challenged in mathematics.

As Tina explained, "Collaboration, communication, and keeping up to date with what's going on were key." She worked on these skills both inside and outside of her middle school by being a part of the group that attended statewide seminars and stayed up-to-date on the new acceleration guidelines.

She also learned about the importance of communicating with the high school. For example, she learned that although their middle school was the largest of the feeder schools, they were not sending any students to the high school for geometry. Yet another smaller district was sending 10–12 students. Tina recognized that their middle schoolers could participate in the high school geometry program and expressed feeling "like we were holding students back a little bit." She reflected on how sometimes educators can be overly protective, believing that students can't do something (e.g., they can't go to the high school as an eighth grader). But she pushed back, saying, "Everyone's doing it, why not our kids?"

Tina believes that if teachers aim high, students will aim higher: "I truly feel that if you push students and ask them to do things they are capable of, they will surprise." Aiming higher also means pushing into more conceptual mathematics and integrating processes like writing. For example, Tina shared an interaction she had with a teacher who was reluctant to integrate writing into mathematics. She had asked, "Hey, how's that writing coming along?" Then later she whispered into the reading teacher's ear, "Can you get into that classroom and help her out with some writing?" Tina summarized her leadership approach: "You push, push, nudge, nudge. We will all get there."

MEGHAN EVERETTE, MATH COACH AND POWERED BY TEACH TO LEAD SUMMIT COORDINATOR, SALT LAKE CITY, UTAH

Meghan is a teacher in the Salt Lake City School District, serving as a teacher specialist in K–6 mathematics, which equates to a math coach. Megan provides services to two Title I schools: a K–6 school and a K–5 school. Both schools house preschool programs, though they are limited in size. Meghan is on a teaching contract and is a teacher on special assignment.

There are 35,000 students in the district of Salt Lake City; however, it is not the largest school district in the state. Salt Lake is a minority/majority school district. "Many of the students are refugees," Meghan explained. Meghan reported that at one of her schools, 26 different languages are spoken. In all, 90 different languages are spoken in the Salt Lake district. Meghan noted that while there are many different languages spoken, Spanish is still the most frequently used, but one could also find languages like Somali, Tongan, Burmese, Bosnian, Vietnamese, and Chinese.

Meghan described her district as an urban school district that is centrally located in the state. The district is a public school district, but it also includes charter schools that each operate a little differently. For example, one is art-based; another is science- and-math-based. When one travels about an hour and a half in any direction, the state landscape is very remote and scarcely populated.

There is a noticeable divide between the east and west sides of the city. The east side of Salt Lake City is composed of more middle- to upper-class families. The east side is also where the university is located. In contrast, the west side of the city houses primarily Title I schools. Both of Meghan's schools are located on the west side. Each of the schools in which Meghan works has about 500 students. There are about three teachers at each grade level, and the schools boast full inclusion.

When asked about teacher leadership in the district, Meghan shared her past experience as a teacher leader and how Salt Lake is more formal: "Interestingly, Salt Lake is a shared government district. In other words, each school has a high level of independence. And it has been like that for a long time—since 1974." Meghan went on to say that this independence meant each school in the district looked a little different from the others.

While all of the schools are required to have a certain number of hours and days, parent-teacher conferences, and start and end times, each school is arranged differently via a school-based team that includes not only the principal but a team of teachers. Meghan shared:

> Reps (representatives from each of the grade level teams) are kind of considered the building leadership. The school reps come together and are the voice of the teachers. . . . So, each school arranges their day differently based on the decisions of the school leadership team. Each school also sets up their team differently. For example, you can volunteer, or have a teacher from each grade level be on the team. The principal tries not to overload anyone with too much.

Meghan noted that there were two other teams, a student service team and a school improvement team, but that there were no contractual arrangements for those teams and their meetings. Meghan added, "If you have three teachers at a grade level in a school, one might serve on each team." However, she said that while leaders rotate at her school every year, in other schools they have a leader on a committee, and membership stays that way indefinitely. Moreover, if principals want to advance an innovative initiative, the idea must first go through the school's leadership team.

The next level of teacher leaders is the coaching level. The coaches work with teachers and design and deliver professional development in the district. The coaching position is not administrative or evaluative. Still, the coaching positions are seen as leadership roles, and teachers have to apply for a role as a coach. There are science coaches, math, English language arts, English language development, and also peer-assisted review coaches. The peer-assisted review coach is a little different, as teachers have to be in the district for five years before they can apply for this coaching position, which includes an evaluative role, whereas the other coaching positions do not.

Meghan came into her coaching position from out of state and worked on her math endorsement as she served in the math coach role. The district requires an English as a Second Language (ESL) endorsement. While Meghan did not have the endorsement when she applied for the coaching position, she had many other strengths that were valued. Meghan has presented at the national level, has experience designing professional development, and has worked with her previous state on standards and standards alignment.

In 2018, Meghan was finishing both math and ESL endorsements and was enrolled in a doctoral program in curriculum and instruction in teaching and teacher education. She liked the curriculum and instruction side of her current work and enjoyed doing professional development with teachers. Her leadership role required her to work 10 extra days beyond the teacher calendar.

Meghan described her role in this way: "I'm usually a week at one school and a week at the other school. They're just a block apart so I can go back and forth if emergencies arise." In her current coaching position, Meghan does instructional cycles with teachers. She meets to plan ahead of time, co-teaches, observes, and shares feedback. Meghan also assists with planning and sits in on professional learning community meetings. Professional learning communities are teacher led, used to look at data to inform instruction, and develop common and formative assessments:

> Each coach is a lead on completing a particular grade level. Leads usually create district common formative assessments that are reviewed by the entire coaching team, work on the grade-level pacing guides, end-of-level assessments, or teach supplemental grade-level cohort classes. . . . We focus on what good math classes look like using videotaping and talking about what works and what doesn't. . . . Each teacher videotapes what they've worked on and then reviews the videotape using guided reflection and discussion on what works. Then we goal set for the next time.

Meghan explained that teachers from other schools, not just her own, can choose whether they want to participate and earn continuing education class credit. They also receive $600 for the year if they attend eight two-hour sessions. These professional development opportunities are made possible through a grant that the Salt Lake District Teaching and Learning Department received. The coaches develop the content based on student/school/district need.

Meghan is considered a teacher specialist, although other districts might call her a coach. As a teacher specialist Meghan works with teachers and helps them develop interventions, but she also works on best practices, which could be pacing, student engagement, or math concepts. Meghan might also work with teachers outside of the classroom such as PLCs, in planning, 1:1, modeling, co-teaching, observing, or giving feedback.

The project Meghan is most proud of is the one that she completed in the summer of 2018. Meghan worked with another teacher and hosted a state summit for Powered By Teach to Lead. Teach to Lead hosts national summits around the country. A teacher has an idea about how to improve teaching and learning, then applies to Teach to Lead to bring forth the idea. If accepted, the teacher puts together a team to go to the summit, where participants develop an action plan. Powered By Teach to Lead is an offshoot at the local or regional level. Meghan applied and took a team to a national Teach to Lead summit, where she learned about Powered By Teach to Lead.

Meghan's project was at the state level. The summit was designed to help teams develop action plans and implement their projects. As Utah was interested in mathematics and equity, Meghan and a colleague focused on how they could engage teams of educators around this focus. When her colleague got the go-ahead from the state, Meghan reached out to Celeste Rodriguez and others at the Department of Education.

Meghan completed an application for a Powered By Teach to Lead summit. Once approved, she set out to design the Powered By Teach to Lead summit for 100 teachers from all over the state. All of the teams had to apply to address an issue in one of three areas: high-quality instruction that was either team-based or data-based problem solving; special populations—inclusion-Tier One or access to grade-level content; or co-teaching, co-planning and collaboration. Each team had to commit to the whole two-day summit, bring a team (up to five people) in which teachers were central, and agree to work with a critical friend who was identified by Meghan and the planning team. Teams at every grade level from K–2 to university participated, and the teams included technology as well as content faculty.

In the Utah Powered By Teach to Lead summit that Meghan coordinated, teams came in and were guided through the different steps of developing their action plan with strategic questions designed to get to the root of the issue. Meghan described the process as kind of a backward design. Each team developed the steps, the strategies and resources, as well as the timing for their plan. The summit included a teacher leader speaker, a student performance, and focused breakouts to develop each team's plan. Toward the end of day two, each team hung up their giant poster plan, and then the teams all participated in a gallery walk to ask questions and provide feedback for each other. Finally, the team met and went over all of the questions and feedback from others to strengthen their plan.

Meghan said that as a follow-up to the two-day summit, the teams were participating in blogs and state meetings to talk about what they were doing with their projects. Meghan explained that they did not have any formal way to bring everyone back together, but as the state was partnered with the summit, the projects would be discussed at state math meetings, and teams were invited to talk about and provide evidence at various state meetings. While no conclusive evidence was available at the time of the interview, the summit facilitated teacher teams in creating action plans to address math equity and inclusion in Utah, a critical state conversation.

Meghan continued, "The summit created lots of excitement and showed the commitment of teachers who were willing to come during the summer and work to flush out big ideas." The state superintendent spoke and was really excited about seeing teachers and leaders engaged in purposeful work during the summer. His enthusiasm was key to igniting others.

Since the summit Meghan has heard from people who are implementing their projects. Meghan has been excited to learn that they are doing their project work and using it as a way to talk to principals about community needs, talk to other teachers, and collaborate.

Meghan explained that the summit was important because teachers across the state needed time and a structure to work on really hard problems. "This is a big deficit in teaching and learning in the United States. In other countries teachers have time to collaborate and work together," Meghan noted. She went on to state that teachers and coaches often have ideas, but they just don't have time and space to work on solutions to address critical problems. "The summit made that possible and people really got excited about working on this because big problems became attainable. Teachers had a space to be leaders and be a part of the solution." Meghan said that teachers she knew had not had anything like the summit in professional development in Salt Lake or anywhere in the state—maybe not even the country.

The biggest challenge to this project was time. Meghan said time is always an issue, especially when organizing the summit and supporting all teachers in all districts with an opportunity to participate. That's why they held the event at the end of July and the beginning of August. The summit actually started the school year for some of the districts. Travel was also challenging because the state is very rural. To reach out to the whole state, they had to find the right people.

Many groups provided assistance that helped to make the summit successful. Support came from Teach to Lead, the Utah Teacher Fellows, and the state. Teach to Lead provided templates to do the work, as well as personnel. And the Utah Teacher Fellows helped secure food donations for meals and snacks and also helped with general setup and promotion. The state funded travel and lodging for people who were more than 50 miles away. Meghan wanted people to feel welcomed, and feedback from the event supported the idea that the participants felt like professionals and that the lodging, travel, food, and snacks really helped to achieve those feelings.

> As for me, this project really developed my understanding of the state and districts across the state. I feel like I am now able to reach out and talk to the state agency and that is huge. I just really understand the state and its obstacles and resources and what is going on in the schools so much better.

Meghan emphasized the idea that the amount of professional development she had engaged in—not the mandatory professional development where everyone does the same thing, but rather the different things she'd been able to do—had made her want to network and access those networks for other teachers. "A lot of teachers don't get to go outside their school, and they don't know what else is out there. They should know. It's important and eye opening," affirmed Meghan. "I want to provide those experiences for other teachers."

All of Meghan's experiences made her feel very confident. She felt like she was both supported and connected, and it made her feel like she could do anything. Yet Meghan's experiences also made her aware of all that she doesn't know. Meghan explained that her own children, as well as the students in her classroom, reminded her that she is always a learner "and like the teachers I work with, I have to go above and beyond for all of them—to advantage them as others have advantaged me. I get as much as I give."

Meghan laughingly said that her goal should be to learn how to say 'No,' but she just has a lot of interests and so it is hard for her to stay focused on just one issue. Meghan is passionate about advocacy, not just student advocacy, but teacher advocacy. As Meghan works on her dissertation, teacher advocacy is her focus. Meghan would like to be a National School Ambassador Fellow for the Department of Education. "I wouldn't make that a career, but it is my dream." Meghan wants to remain in the classroom. When she is not in the classroom, she misses it. Meghan also loves curriculum and instruction, policy, and advocacy, so perhaps she'll work with an educational organization. For Meghan, "policy and advocacy are too removed from the classroom. I think that is a big problem for us today." But not for long with Meghan advancing as a teacher leader.

TERI BALDWIN, KINDERGARTEN TEACHER AND UNION PRESIDENT, PALO ALTO, CALIFORNIA

Theresa (Teri) Baldwin has been a kindergarten teacher for 22 of her 24 years of teaching. While she began teaching in Connecticut, she now teaches in California. Teri explained that she attended a traditional teacher preparation program at University of Connecticut and earned both a bachelor's and master's degree in education. "What was unique about my program," said Teri, "was that my bachelors program was a five year program. My masters degree then provided a concentration in a particular area like technology." Teri explained that this was limiting because the candidates didn't have the experience to know what or whom they might want to teach.

Teri teaches kindergarten in a neighborhood school with a student population of 475 students. Over time her school has become a Title I school, meaning that it receives some additional federal funding because of subsidized public housing in the attendance area. The district houses 12 elementary schools, 3 middle schools, 2 high schools, and an adult school.

Teri's school boasts a student teacher ratio of 17:1. According to state test scores, 78% of the students are proficient in math and 80% in reading. Sixty-one percent of the students are Caucasian, 14% Asian, 13% dual race, 9% Hispanic and 3% other. Five percent of the students are eligible for free lunch, and 2% are eligible for reduced lunch.

Teri is on full release from the classroom, as she is president of her school district's union, serving 900 teachers and 19 school sites. In this position, Teri is on a teacher contract; 50% of her salary comes from the district and 50% comes from the union. Teri's district is affiliated with the California Teachers Association, an affiliate of the National Education Association.

In her position as president, Teri is in charge of maintaining her members' wages, benefits, and working conditions. She has to be in constant contact with her site representatives to understand how policies, curriculum, and new procedures are being implemented in their schools to ensure fidelity. As president, Teri advocates for all of the teachers' rights and works to address grievances and inform administrators of problems. She also attends board meetings and keeps abreast of committee workings and initiatives throughout the district.

Teri became interested in union work during her first teaching assignment in her first teaching position. Teri shared, "While I don't remember how I got to my first union meeting, what I do recall is that there was an unjust situation occurring amongst the teachers."

In this district, professional development days were not mandatory, and the teachers were not paid for the time they invested. "Nevertheless, the vast majority of teachers attended the professional development days without pay." However, that year the superintendent sent a letter that suggested that all the teachers had better attend, and that they weren't very professional if they didn't attend. The tone of the letter was insulting, and the union took a vote about attending.

The vote was decisive, and action was taken. There would be a no show for the professional development days until the teachers received pay for them. While the teachers believed that professional development was important, they argued that the current policy was socially unjust and that professionals should always get paid for their time. Teri got involved with organizing and disseminating information in the community, and this is how she began to get involved in policy and union work.

When Teri moved to California and her new kindergarten position, she maintained her membership in the union and got involved in her local unit. "I started speaking up at meetings and then people started asking for my opinion. Other people helped me see the importance of my voice and that encouraged me."

Teri held many roles that advanced her knowledge of policy and developed her leadership voice, including site representative and lead negotiator. But Teri said, "For me, the most important part of being a teacher leader is having the experience and confidence in being a teacher. That confidence and the success I had with students helped me to see that I was a leader."

Teri also said, "I went into being a union president with 18 years of teaching experience and 12 years of experience in the union as site representative and lead negotiator." Prior to becoming president of her union, Teri was elected vice president. When the call came for a new person to fill the role of president, Teri answered the call. To become president, Teri threw her name into the ring, and the entire membership voted. Winning a majority of the votes, Teri became the union president in her school district.

While all of her involvement in union activities paved the way for her to become president, Teri explained that her state affiliation also provided a four- to five-day training program during the summer for presidents each year along with some daylong conference meetings. Teri participated in the training for several years as she established herself as president of her local union. Initially, Teri taught one day a week and had four release days to engage in the duties of the union president, but in 2018 she was granted a full release.

Teri explained that one of the most meaningful projects she worked on as union president also involved her passion for teaching kindergarten. The district wanted to unify access and opportunity for students in kindergarten and move from an extended-day to a full-day program for all kindergarten students across the district. This extended-day program was created for small group and individualized instruction and had a schedule in which all students came to school in the mornings and half the students stayed after lunch for a one-hour extended-day program on Mondays and Tuesdays and the others stayed for their extended days on Thursday and Fridays. All students stayed all day on Wednesdays, a district-wide early-release day. Not all the kindergarten teachers were in favor of this change, which was supported by parents and administrators.

Community and teacher meetings ensued, and there was concern among some veteran kindergarten teachers about both student learning and teacher working conditions. Teri provided a sounding board and a voice for the teachers and worked with the school board, administration, and community to find a compromise that would be mutually beneficial:

> Some teachers wanted to keep the small group instruction we had in the extended day program. I attended multiple meetings, was still a kindergarten teacher and listened to all of the teachers. As I realized some research was supporting a full day compared to half day program and that was the direction the district would move, I worked to negotiate a compromise that would address their concerns. The compromise included reduced class size—19—and contractual aide time in the classroom to ensure that students' individual needs could still be met even in a full day program. It also included training time and time to discuss what worked.

Teri gathered information from the California Teacher Association and talked to other districts and other presidents to find relevant research and work in districts across the state. While research and data were shared at the meetings, a challenge in the process was getting the teachers who opposed the change to feel that they were listened to and heard. So the key role that Teri played was bringing the teacher concerns forward at all of the meetings:

> In terms of outcomes I think the teachers know that they have someone who is there for them. As for student outcomes, we haven't seen the academic growth we thought we might see, but it is still a new initiative and the data is largely anecdotal. While some teachers think what we are doing is wonderful, not all agree and there are some concerns about social and emotional growth. For me, I learned about the importance of getting out to the teachers more often and listening to their concerns.

Teri's work impacted 36 kindergarten classrooms across the district. And though some of the kindergarten teachers were not completely happy with the move to full day, they appreciated their concerns being heard as the compromise specifically addressed their concerns.

Teri reported that there are basically two different ways to be a leader in her current district. "You can be a union site representative, or at one time you could be a lead teacher for each of the disciplines, like a math lead and so on." Teri noted that because of tight budgets the lead teacher position was replaced with a TOSA. There are three TOSAs at the elementary level, and four at the middle and high school levels.

Site representatives teach on a regular contract and do not receive any release time. The representatives receive training through the union that is encouraged but not mandated. To be a site representative, a teacher just expresses an interest.

TOSAs go into the schools to provide information about programs, answer questions, and provide training. TOSA leaders are on a teacher contract. TOSAs are not negotiated but rather are identified as a role that teachers apply for. They work a little bit longer on the calendar year and are compensated per a teachers' contract. There is no special training in the district for a TOSA, but in the interview process, particular content and skills are examined.

"I'm struggling with what I will do next," reported Teri. Her plan was to go back into the classroom. "In the district there is no place higher for me to go than being the union president, but I may get my administrative credential." Teri doesn't want to be a principal but she would like to lead education back to being more developmentally oriented.

Teri never intended to be a union president, but she does enjoy being able to help her colleagues. Other areas she sees as important in growing her leadership include learning to delegate some responsibilities so that she can conserve time to help others develop their leadership skills and grow more leaders.

> I've realized over time that teaching is a noble profession and that teachers who are at the forefront of education have to be a voice for students—an advocate. I know that as a teacher leader—in or out of the classroom—I can both advocate and help others advocate for students, teachers and education policy.

While Teri doesn't think her leadership experience will change how she teaches in the classroom, she does plan to do more advocating for her students and colleagues and for all students and programs in her school district. "I realize that as a teacher I can't just rely on the union and its executive board, but that I as a teacher need to be a voice."

SUMMARY

In this chapter we find four cases of teachers on special assignment, from assessment coordinator, the role that Jodie embodies, to union president, Teri's role. The manner in which each assignment came about is novel and demonstrates the unique thinking, interests, experiential background, and resourcefulness of each teacher leader.

A number of stakeholders were involved in each case and that complicated the work that each teacher leader undertook. Note how each teacher leader navigated the spectrum of stakeholders to intentionally engage each group and build community to garner support for the work to be done.

Ultimately each teacher leader advocated for her cause, though each defined her success in a unique way. To achieve success, the teacher leaders accessed a variety of resources that played an important role in each endeavor. Teri, for example, met with the kindergarten teachers at each of the elementary schools in her district, but she also met with the administration, parents in the community, and school board members to learn about and understand the perspectives that each group brought to the decision-making table. While the option she represented was not chosen at that time, she established a communication channel with her colleagues and with other groups that allowed all stakeholders to see they had a voice at the table, and that was a win!

As you reflect on the leadership of each educator highlighted in this chapter, consider other parts of the Framework (Strike, Fitzsimmons, & Hornberger, 2019). Read chapter 8 to further explore ways to analyze the impact of each case study. Pay close attention to the teacher leaders' decisions and the opportunities or challenges that their unique contexts afforded. Evaluate the ways in which you might have approached the situations presented in these cases or similar situations in your teaching context.

Finally, note the reverence and passion each teacher exudes for teaching and learning. And of course, see that central to each case is the welfare of the student.

REFLECTIVE QUESTIONS AND APPLICATION

1. Who are the primary stakeholders in each of these cases? The secondary stakeholders? Are any disenfranchised? How did the teacher leaders engage them?
2. How do teacher leaders in these cases build community to collaborate with all of the stakeholders? How will you collaborate with all the stakeholders

involved with your project? What engagement will you have with those indirectly impacted by your project?

3. For what or for whom are the teacher leaders in these cases advocating? For what or for whom will you advocate?

4. What unique resources does each teacher leader bring to her case? What is your project? What resources will you both need and bring to support your advocacy?

REFERENCES

Ranch View Middle School. (2018). *Response to intervention.* Retrieved from https://rvms.dcsdk12.org/our_school/more_rvms_programming/response_to_intervention

Strike, K., Fitzsimmons, J., & Hornberger, R. (2019). *Identifying and growing internal leaders: A framework for effective teacher leadership.* Lanham, MD: Rowman & Littlefield.

Chapter Eight

Case Study Analysis

Formal case study analysis is important for advancing critical thinking and problem solving as teacher leaders. In this book, problem-oriented cases are presented to share challenges and opportunities across a variety of contexts with an array of teacher leaders. A problem-oriented case study (PCS) is "analyzed to identify the major problems that exist and suggest solutions to these problems" (Monash University Library, 2018, p. 1). A PCS reflects authentic situations where theory and practice are interrelated, a problem is identified, solutions are shared, and details for implementation are outlined. Challenges and findings are recognized and outlined without going into depth.

Across the chapters, case studies were chosen to provide examples for better understanding and developing teacher leadership knowledge, skills, and dispositions. Hayes (2000) shared Stake's definition of the case study method as the selection of a specific, unique, bounded system to be investigated. A case can be studied for a variety of reasons. In this book, cases serve as vehicles to investigate educational problems and issues faced by teacher leaders through focusing on a specific leadership challenge. Stake also described how the narrative of the case provides an opportunity for vicarious experience, where readers expand their memories of happenings, leading to increased awareness and understanding (Hayes, 2000).

The use of case studies in teacher education has a long history, being based in the research of educators such as Shulman (1986), who advocated for their use in the same manner that case studies are used to teach the practice of law. Legal educators historically have used case studies not to teach specific instances of the law but to argue for a broad application of how a law works. A particular case stands as a general example of the law in action, and it serves as a model for new applications of that law. Similarly, teacher leader case studies in this book represent generalizable examples of the knowledge, skills, and dispositions of effective leadership across a variety of contexts.

Shulman (1986) suggested that educational case studies could be used similarly to legal cases. He described how case studies representing typical situations might serve as teaching tools to illustrate how teachers apply educational theory to make decisions. Shulman also recommended that teachers should practice the analysis of case studies early in their preparation to begin to apply theory and develop frameworks for thinking through complex problems. These conceptual frameworks will not provide the correct solution to every problem for teachers—that is impossible. However, such case-based problem solving can help teachers by improving their skills in analyzing and organizing experiences. According to Posner (1989), it is the combination of experience and reflection that produces growth and development as a teacher.

Analysis is a higher-order thinking skill, and as a skill it must be practiced. Identifying key practices and pivotal decisions leads to questioning and understanding at a deeper level. This higher-order analysis can be visualized using resources such as Bloom's Taxonomy Wheel or the Depth of Knowledge Wheel. Within Bloom's Taxonomy, analysis is coupled with comparison, differentiation, examination, and investigation. Within the Depth of Knowledge, analysis is Level Four (of the four levels). Here, extended thinking is linked to terms such as *connect*, *visualize*, *critique*, and *synthesize*.

CASE STUDY RESEARCH

In addition to understanding what case analysis calls for, teachers must also understand scholarly inquiry. Through inquiry, scholars present new findings, recent information, or the results of experiments; present new interpretations, speculations, or thoughts; gather together all that is currently known on a subject to see how it fits together and to reach some conclusions; show the relationship of two areas of study; show the light one sheds on the other; and determine the truth of a matter and prove that truth to other researchers (Bazerman, 2010, p. 111).

For many qualitative researchers, case study is the primary method of data collection and reporting. Multiple sources of data are used in case study research, including interviews, observations, artifacts, and documents chosen to provide deep insight into the specifics of a specific case. Emphasis is placed on examining an event, problem, process, activity, program, single person, or group. The case study takes place within a bounded system with boundaries such as time, space, or place.

Therefore, through scholarly writing and application of higher-order thinking skills, case study analysis is an excellent research methodology and learning tool to evaluate programs; establish interventions; obtain vivid insight; generate and evaluate alternatives; develop an action plan; and further understand, develop, and test theory. Through analysis one can specifically look at improvement; mission; strategies; resources (cost, return, materials, personnel, time); risks and returns; effectiveness; implementation; morale; safety; turnover; flexibility; attitudes, stereotypes, or prejudices; and impact. The case study analysis aims to investigate, examine, and propose.

Hayes (2000) identified Searle's four advantages of case study analysis as stimulating new research, contradicting established theory, giving new insight into phenomena or experience, and permitting investigation of otherwise inaccessible situations. Other advantages of case studies are their setting in a natural environment and context; the researcher being able to ask questions for clarification or delve deeper; and the flexibility to make immediate revisions or further exploration in the future. Case study research allows specifying gaps or holes in existing theory with the ultimate goal of advancing theoretical explanations, and Eisenhardt's (1989) ideal of no theory first captures the richness of observation without being limited by a theory. Eisenhardt (1989) pointed out that:

> The process involves the use of multiple investigators and multiple data collection methods as well as a variety of cross-case searching tactics. Each of these tactics involves viewing evidence from diverse perspectives. However, the process also involves converging on construct definitions, measures, and a framework for structuring the findings. Finally, the process [described here] is intimately tied with empirical evidence. Case study analysis encourages curiosity and exploration of anomalies in prior theories not to reject but to further explore. (p. 546)

Case study methodology examines effective teacher leadership through reflection focused on philosophy, theory, research, and subject matter needed to make informed and professional decisions. Case study analysis calls for identification, description, analysis, and problem solving. When analyzing case studies, both reader and developer must adhere to protective policies of both the district and federal legislation called the Family Education Rights and Privacy Act (FERPA), which provides guidelines about who can have access to student records and when written permission is required to view records.

According to Campoy (2005), data collection occurs through and should reflect three main categories: observation, interview, and documents. Observation includes the use of instruments, forms, sheets, running records, narratives, commercial forms, teacher-created forms, checklists, surveys and questionnaires, open-ended questions, structured (multiple choice) questions, the Likert scale, audiotape, videotape, and photographs.

Data collection through interview includes individual or focus groups, open-ended or running record, structured or semi-structured, audiotaped with transcription, or videotaped with transcription. Subjects include but are not limited to students, teachers, specialists, counselors, school nurse, administrators, and parents.

Documents reviewed in case study analysis include but are not limited to standardized test results, diagnostic test results, individualized education plans (IEPs) and 504 plans, teacher-created assessments, common assessments (end-of-unit, end-of-year, etc.), writing samples (rubric), reading assessments (miscue analysis, decoding, comprehension, etc.), performance tasks (rubric), portfolio (rubric), project-based learning (rubric), oral presentation (rubric), school records, minutes of meetings, attendance records, detention records, progress reports (report cards), student monitoring (MAP data), classroom and school newsletters, and photographs.

Legalities call for attention to records policies and permission to conduct the case study. However, there are other aspects specific to ethics: protecting the privacy of case study subjects through the use of pseudonyms; the requirement to not divulge any information that might prove harmful or embarrassing to a student, classroom, school, district, or colleague; and the condition to not discuss the case study outside of the context provided regardless of the level of information sought.

Disadvantages identified by Searle include researcher bias or the influence of the researcher's personal interpretation influencing the data; memory distortion or change of data based on the memory of the person(s) providing the data; lack of replication since the data are specific to that one person; and low reliability based on measure(s) chosen (Hayes, 2000). Another disadvantage is that identification of boundaries of each case may prove challenging. Also, the process of finding a case and studying it, or addressing an issue and then matching a case to study, can be difficult to ascertain. Finally, in studying multiple case studies, the researcher may lose data or not go as deep into each case individually (Flipp, 2014).

Three methods of analysis are encouraged in the case study design. First is intrinsic or within-case analysis. The researcher provides material in a descriptive, thorough manner which one can then interpret, draw one's own conclusions, and create generalizations based on one's own experiences. Here the reader searches for emerging constructs and relationships. Second is instrumental or across-case analysis, in which the reader understands phenomena and relationships, categorically aggregates the data, and examines the phenomenon across several cases. Here the reader learns through analysis of the case and aggregation of the data. The third method is to generate assertions or interpretation of the meaning of the data, identify themes, and construct lessons from the data. Here the reader searches for patterns and generalizations.

CLOSE READING OF A CASE STUDY

Important to the process is close reading of the case studies. Close reading requires multiple reads to deconstruct and reconstruct the case study, looking for key ideas, patterns, and details. It also requires the use of critical questions to develop a deep, precise understanding of the case studies. The use of critical questions is important for exploring a particular case, comparing the case with other cases in this book, and utilizing the cases to their fullest teaching potential. To support the close reading of cases within a chapter, each chapter begins with the rubric focused on selected elements of *Identifying and Growing Internal Leaders: A Framework for Effective Teacher Leadership* (Strike, Fitzsimmons, & Hornberger, 2019). However, these rubrics are applicable to cases in other chapters as well.

First Read: Key Ideas and Context

The first read may be done independently, as a read aloud, think aloud, paired, or shared reading. The first read should allow the reader to focus on key ideas and details without building or integrating background. The reader may annotate the case study with these big ideas and identify gaps in information, note any connections to research and resources focused on teacher leadership, or note connections to other cases in this book. For example, the reader might identify critical competencies in teacher leadership, such as engaging all stakeholders, valuing and drawing upon the culture and community they serve.

Critical questions for a first read may include: What are the facts here? What do I know? What do I not know and have questions about? What are the big ideas about teacher leadership being shared? What is confusing? What information is needed? What can I infer about the person(s) or institution? Who are the main characters? What stands out to me? Who is presenting this case? How do this person's background characteristics, personal viewpoints, and professional experiences shape the case study? Whose stories were told? Which stories were left untold? What perspectives are missing?

Second Read: Notations and Coding

A second read focuses on complex elements or ideas to further explore to arrive at a deeper understanding of the text. The second read should allow the reader to share thoughts with a partner or in small groups. The second read may further explore vocabulary, key ideas, and the use of marginal notes and coding. For example, an exclamation mark may be used where a reader notes similarities to his/her own placement or experience, or a question mark where there is a lack of familiarity between author and reader.

Critical questions for a second read may include: What is the problem-solution relationship being presented? Were there multiple problems that needed an integrated solution? Were there multiple solutions to a single problem? Identify the problem and the solution being presented in the case study. What similarities and differences are notable in the case study shared and your own experience? How does your own point of view compare to the author's? Which factors are the most important characteristics for understanding this case study? What contextual influences were central to the case's problem and solution?

Third Read: Integration of Knowledge and Ideas

The third read of a text requires the reader to go deeper to synthesize and analyze information from several resources and background experience. The reader may record ideas on sticky notes, in a graphic organizer, or with another organizational method of choice.

Critical questions for a third read may include: What were the most important teacher leader knowledge, skills, dispositions, and practices in this case study? What were other courses of action this teacher leader might have taken? Whose perspectives are being shared in the case study? How might these perspectives be challenged? Whose perspectives are silent but need voice? Were there other possible solutions that might have been more inclusive or collaborative or have resulted in a more positive impact on students? What administrative or leadership theories were represented in the case? What conceptual frameworks were helpful for understanding the case study?

Additional critical questions for the third read include: What were the resource implications surrounding the central problem in the case study, or how did finances impact the chosen solution? What measurable costs are there to the proposed solution, and what are the costs if the problem is not addressed? What human and material resources were essential in the decision-making process? What were the risks that each teacher leader took in attempting to solve the problem? Did the teacher leader experience any reservations prior to, during, or following planning or implementation of the project? What did the teacher leader learn through this project? How had his/her prior experience and knowledge base contributed to his/her professional development? How did the teacher leader empower others?

The primary purpose of a close reading is to revisit the case multiple times for different purposes. For example, returning to a case study after reading subsequent case studies that seemed to share a theme or basic principle would give new purpose to the rereading.

WRITING A CASE BRIEF

A common way to formalize the analysis of a case study is to write a brief. The idea of a brief comes from the legal field, in which law students learn to write briefs after reading a legal case. A similar format can be followed for a written analysis of an educational case study, and briefs can be very useful in oral presentations or discussions of cases. Student case briefs can be extensive or short, depending on the depth of analysis required and the purpose of the case study.

A common form of case brief is the student brief. Student briefs are given as assignments so the written analyses of the case studies can be used in class discussions, and the briefs can be revisited and used as comparisons to new cases. Using an adaptation of the instructions from the Lloyd Sealy Library (2017) at the John Jay College of Criminal Justice, the following seven parts for writing educational case study briefs are suggested:

1. Title and citation.
2. Facts of the case: Write a one-sentence description of the case and then introduce the key characteristics of the case using quotes from the case study. Finally, briefly summarize the problem the case presented and the solution described.
3. Issues: In law the issues are domain specific, such as issues of law or procedural issues. In education the issues will be conceptually different and reflect important topics for discussion related to working with schools, such as curricular issues, logistical issues, issues of authority or power, issues of trust or collaboration, community issues, etc. A complex case study may illustrate more than one issue, but the brief should describe the issues most relevant to the case.
4. Decisions: In law the decisions, or holding, is the court's decision. In an educational study the decisions made are the solution paths chosen to solve problems. Decision options might need to be inferred from the action steps taken, if there is no clear description of the decision path.

5. Reasoning: The reasoning section in a law brief is the section that summarizes the rationale(s) given by the judge(s). In an educational case study brief, the reasoning would be a brief outline of the case study teacher's logic in drawing the case to the stated conclusion. For example, because A occurred, the educator had to X in order to accomplish Y and reach the goal of Z. The chain of reasoning may parallel the decision pathway, but it is distinct from it.

6. Separate opinions: Obviously in a law brief this section is used when the judges give different opinions in deciding a case. In an educational brief this is the section of the brief in which an alternative perspective should be presented. Do you agree with the decisions and reasoning of the case study educator? What are areas of disagreement? What are other ways of looking at this case?

7. Analysis: The final section in a law school student brief is the analysis section, in which the student judges the significance of a case. In an educational case study brief, use this section to articulate the big ideas or takeaways from this case (e.g., this case is a good example of ___). Also consider how this case is similar to or in contrast with another case study as part of an analysis.

WRITING A CASE STUDY

Writing a case study is an excellent way to evaluate student learning and discuss an assignment as a whole class. It requires analytical and critical thinking processes similar to reading and analysis, may draw upon real experience but present fictional situations, poses a problem with no absolute or obvious answer, requires problem solving and decision making, requires the reader to use information to move to resolution, evaluates the problem and potential solutions, and provides enough information for a good analysis (Lynn, 1999).

There are typically eight sections in a written case study:

1. Introduction: The introduction defines the problem to be examined and explains the parameters or limitations of the situation.

2. Synopsis: The synopsis identifies key issues and provides detail about the 5 Ws (who, what, when, where, and why). It may also identify professional, technical, or theoretical issues and include graphic or visual aids such as budgets, organizational charts, mission statements, or technical specifications as relevant. This section also outlines issues and findings of the case study without the specific details. Here, the reader should be able to get a clear picture of the essential contents of the study and note any assumptions made.

3. Analysis/Findings: In this section the author identifies the problems found in the case. Each analysis of a problem should be supported by facts given in the case together with the relevant theory and course concepts. Here, it is important to search for the underlying problems; for example, cross-cultural conflict may be only a symptom of the underlying problem of inadequate policies and practices within the institution. This section is often divided into subsections, one for each problem.

4. Discussion: This section summarizes the major problem(s) and identifies alternative solutions to this/these major problem(s). Alternative solutions should be evaluated in terms of advantages and disadvantages as well as new issues and possibilities.

5. Conclusion: This section sums up the main points from the findings and discussion.

6. Recommendations: Here the writer provides a list of recommendations based on the case and supported by the professional literature, that is, improving critical competencies, professional growth, advocacy, or instructional leadership. The writer should briefly justify the choice, explaining how it will solve the major problem(s) and integrate theory and resources as appropriate. This should be written in a forceful style, as this section is intended to be persuasive.

7. Implementation: This section identifies what should be done, by whom, and by when. If appropriate include a rough estimate of costs (financial, materials, personnel, and time).

8. References: All references should be accurately cited.

9. Appendices (optional): Any original data that relate to the study but would have interrupted the flow of the main body should be included in the appendices.

Ray McCandless noted that students will be faced with unique problems every day. Solving them depends not only on theory and practice but on creativity and innovative thinking (as cited in Lang, 2011). McCandless recommended reading case studies with a critical eye, reading about writing case studies, engaging in backward mapping to ensure getting out of the experience what is envisioned, and not doing it if it won't be fun (Lang, 2011).

PRESENTING A CASE STUDY

Case studies can be used as presentations to a large or small group and follow a format similar to a written case study brief. A case study presentation has the added opportunity to utilize multimedia and provide a richer context and authentic examples of the facts. While a presentation may follow an outline

Presentation Component	Multimedia Examples
Facts	• Facts can be presented using artifacts from a real case or artifacts that parallel the case study. • Facts can be provided in video or audio only. • Additional information collected on the case study's major components can be shared (e.g., relevant websites, curricular materials).
Problem	• The problem can be stated from different stakeholder perspectives using quotations, audio, or video • Background materials can be presented or linked to (e.g., photos, webpages)
Solution Path	• Participants in the case can explain their solution paths in the first person. • A visual or graphic can be used to illustrate the solution path would enhance a presentation; such visuals can show and highlight decision points.
Analysis	• Final analyses of the case study can be linked back to facts, problem, and solution. • Analyses can be presented in visual format (e.g., conceptual maps, models, graphics).

Figure 8.1. Possible multimedia components for case studies.

similar to the writing of a case study or case brief, the types of information that can be shared are expanded in a visual format, as figure 8.1 illustrates.

Presenting case studies can be useful in exposing a group of diverse educators to a variety of case studies and examining them through discussion. For example, among the 24 case studies in this book, presentations of cases from multiple chapters at the same time would be valuable for analyzing components of teacher leadership that are shared across contexts as well as for examining unique contextual differences. Presentation of case studies is also an effective and efficient way to share a personal case study or a case study project, because the presenter will be able to access artifacts that can be integrated into a multimedia presentation.

DISCUSSING CASE STUDIES

While case studies can be effective for individual professional development, discussing cases with others provides an additional opportunity to present personal interpretations; listen to alternate interpretations; and debate facts, problems, and solutions. Essential for any productive case study discussion will be preparation of the participants and discussion leaders.

To fully participate in any case study discussion, participants must be prepared both in terms of the case study analysis and for debating the case. As previously described, a student case brief is an excellent way to prepare for a small group or large group discussion of a case. In addition, everyone will need access to the original text of the case study for reference. However, conceptual preparation is not sufficient. To effectively participate in a case study discussion, participants must be willing to share their thinking in a public forum, which can bring about feelings of vulnerability.

While there is no single best discussion format, there are several options to provide needed structure, especially in early discussions, where participants may feel unfamiliar with the case study method and uncertain of their analysis skills. Figure 8.2 suggests four discussion formats that will be familiar to most educators, but the number of possibilities is almost limitless.

Discussing case studies with others in ways that allow for deeper analysis, being able to support claims, and listening to alternative interpretations is one of the most powerful ways to learn case knowledge. The central questions to these discussions are what effective teacher leaders know and what they are able to do to lead change in their schools.

SUMMARY

Case study analyses are an important part of educator preparation and professional development. Teaching is foremost a case-based profession, like law and medicine. Educators apply their knowledge and skills to specific cases every day, and from these experiences and professional reflections they build case knowledge. Shulman (1986) addressed case knowledge as one of three forms of knowledge: (a) propositional knowledge, (b) case knowledge, and (c) strategic knowledge.

Within case knowledge, Shulman (1986) proposed three types of knowledge that teachers draw upon to solve problems of practice. In precedent case knowledge, Shulman explained how a teacher's past experiences can become important cases for informing current actions (i.e., Shulman's precedents). With prototype case knowledge, teachers learn to apply theoretical principles through a memorable case example. Third, Shulman described the parable case, in which teachers learn about the norms and values within practice through a story that illuminates these lessons. According to Shulman, case knowledge is used in tandem with knowledge of key principles (i.e., propositions) and strategic knowledge to enhance professional decision making.

Important in case study analysis is how the case study is used to generate discussion among educators. Dialogic interaction is critical to case-based knowledge and learning. Whether the case study is generated by a third party

	Participants	Discussion Leader
Fishbowl	A small group discusses the case in a center circle while the larger class listens and takes notes in a larger surrounding circle. Modification. Setting up a chat room for the larger circle will increase involvement and can be used by the discussion leader to interject questions or raise issues.	• Choosing small group participants, • Preparing Socratic questions and guiding the inner circle discussion, and • Debriefing the case discussion by integrating the analysis of the larger outside group.
Jigsaw	In small groups of 3-5 participants, members are assigned roles they will use in the case discussion. Roles could be: • the parts of a case or brief (e.g., statement of problem, solution) • actions to perform (e.g., ask probing questions, ensure equitable participation)	• Organizing groups • Deciding on roles and their assignments, and • Debriefing the large group by structuring a sharing out of discussions and synthesizing of group reports.
Point/Counterpoint	1. Participants are divided into small groups and assigned different perspectives on the case. One group is assigned to be the "challengers" (i.e., they will challenge all perspectives). 2. The groups meet to discuss the prepared discussion questions from their perspectives. 3. The room is arranged with a "seat" for each group in a small circle or at a table in the middle. The other group members take seats behind this position and rotate into it after each question.	• Organizing groups and deciding on the perspectives, • Preparing the discussion questions, • Monitoring the discussion and asking for proof from the text when appropriate, and • Leading the large group debrief on the case study.
Socratic Seminar	Participants are seated in a large circle and come prepared to discuss the case using references to the text. They do not raise hands but discuss the case to seek out different possible answers to the questions posed by the Discussion Leader. Important to this method is equitable participation and the use of the case text to support claims. Modification. Use a fishbowl organization with a smaller group circle inside the larger group circle. Participants tap the shoulder of someone in the inner circle to exchange seats with them.	• Preparing Socratic questions, • Monitoring discussion by ensuring equitable participation and support for claims, • Asking questions only as needed, and • Bringing closure to the discussion.

Figure 8.2. Example discussion formats for case studies.

or by one of the educators involved in its discussion, the reading, analysis, and discussion of case studies are an important source of every teacher's professional development.

REFLECTIVE QUESTIONS AND APPLICATION

1. What are some benefits to using case study analysis? What are some challenges or limitations to case study use?
2. What are some ways case study analysis could be effectively used by teacher leaders?
3. Which of the case study analysis methods would be most useful or have been most useful in using this book?
4. How have you adapted some of the suggestions in this chapter to analyze case studies? In what ways have your innovations been useful to understanding teacher leadership?
5. Which approaches or elements of approaches for analyzing case studies lend themselves to deeper-level discussion of teacher leadership? Why?

REFERENCES

Baxter, P., & Jack, S. (2008, December). Qualitative case study methodology: Study design and implementation for novice researchers. *The Qualitative Report, 13*(4), 544–59.

Bazerman, C. (2010). *The informed writer: Using sources in the disciplines* (5th ed.). Fort Collins, CO: The WAC Clearinghouse.

Campoy, R. (2005). *Case study analysis in the classroom: Becoming a reflective teacher.* Thousand Oaks, CA: Sage Publications, Inc.

Eisenhardt, K. (1989, October). Building theories from case study research. *Academy of Management Review, 14*(4), 532–50.

Flipp, C. (2014, February 21). *Case study.* Retrieved from https://www.youtube.com/watch?time_continue=273&v=FuG8AzK9GVQ.

Hayes, N. (2000) *Doing psychological research: Gathering and analysing data.* Buckingham, UK: Open University Press.

Lang, J. (2011, July 5). Teaching student to write a case study. *The Chronicle of Higher Education.* Retrieved from https://www.chronicle.com/article/Teaching -Students-to-Write-a/128097

Lloyd Sealy Library. (2017). *How to brief a case.* Retrieved from https://www.lib .jjay.cuny.edu/how-to/brief-a-case

Lynn, L., Jr. (1999). *Teaching and learning with cases: A guidebook.* New York, NY: Chatham House Publishers of Seven Bridges Press, LLC.

Monash University Library. (2018). *Writing a case study*. Clayton, Australia: Monash University.

Posner, G. J. (1989). *Field experience*. New York, NY: Longman.

Shulman, L. (1986). Those who understand: Knowledge growth in teaching. *Educational Researcher, 15*(2), 4–14.

Strike, K., Fitzsimmons, J., & Hornberger, R. (2019). *Identifying and growing internal leaders: A framework for effective teacher leadership*. Lanham, MD: Rowman & Littlefield.

Appendix

Interview Questions:
Teacher Leadership Case Study Project

SCHOOL CONTEXT

- School type (public, parochial, charter, private—indicate all that apply):
- Grade levels serviced:
- School size:
- Student demographics:
- Location: rural, suburban, urban

TEACHER LEADER

- Formal/informal role(s) as TL
- Preparation
- Years of experience
- Current position

CASE STUDY CONTEXT

- How did this successful teacher leadership "project" come about?
- What was the situation at the time this case study was implemented?
- At what "levels" was the case study done (e.g., grade level, department, team level, school- or district-wide)?

SUMMARY OF CASE STUDY

- How would you summarize the case study for someone briefly (e.g., in elevator talk)?

INTENDED OUTCOMES

- What were the intended outcomes? What did you hope to accomplish?

DETAILED PROCESS

- Describe what took place OR share the action plan that guided you through this process.
- What strategies, tools, and resources were used during this process?
- Discuss some of the challenges and barriers.
- Describe the collaborators and resources that were important for supporting the process.
- Share/describe your supporting data/evidence specific to this process.
- Describe the impact on:
  - student learning,
  - colleagues,
  - school/district, and
  - yourself as teacher leader.
- Is there any additional supporting data/evidence that you can share regarding this impact?

PREPARATION

- How were you prepared to become a teacher leader?

SELF-REFLECTION ON TEACHER LEADERSHIP

- What strengths do you see in your own teacher leadership as contributing to the success of this project?
- What areas for improvement do you see in your teacher leadership?
- How do your experiences as a teacher leader shape how you think about yourself as an educator?
- Who benefits from your teacher leadership?

PROFESSIONAL GOALS

- What are your professional goals? What do you want to be doing in five years?
- How do you see your teacher leadership changing/growing/evolving over the next five years?

Index

Index

About the Authors

Kimberly T. Strike, PhD is professor of education and coordinator of doctoral programs at Southern Wesleyan University in Central, South Carolina. She earned her doctorate at Marquette University in the areas of curriculum, instruction, administration, and supervision, with an emphasis on educational technology. She has provided services to public, parochial, choice, and charter schools as a teacher, teacher leader, principal, director of curriculum and instruction, supervisor of title funds, ELA coordinator in the Regional Office of Education, and professor. Kimberly presented on the companion text *Identifying and Growing Internal Leaders: A Framework for Effective Teacher Leadership* (2019) at Carnegie Foundation's Summit for Improvement in Education (2018) and Critical Questions in Education (2019). In addition to the companion text she has six other publications through Rowman & Littlefield, including *Transforming Professional Practice: A Framework for Effective Leadership* (2nd ed., 2020). Among her accomplishments is receipt of the Albert Nelson Marquis Lifetime Achievement Award (2019), PDK's Distinguished Leader in Education Award (2007), and Educational Ambassador to China (2005). She continues to work with various educational and service programs through local, national, and international channels to advance practice and policy for high-quality programs and effective use of teacher leaders.

Jan Fitzsimmons, PhD has taught at North Central College (NCC) since 1985, where she received the college's Dissinger Award for excellence in teaching and performance of a job above and beyond the call of duty. In addition to her teaching duties, she is the founder and executive director of the NCC Urban Education Laboratory, which is home to the Junior/Senior Scholars Program and the Promise Teacher Corps. The Junior/Senior Scholars Program has twice been named an exemplary practice by the Illinois Board of Higher Education. In addition, Jan founded and continues to direct the Center for Success in High-Need Schools, a collaboration of twenty-three independent colleges and universities that come together monthly to advance recruiting, preparing, and retaining teachers and leaders for at-risk schools. She has worked collaboratively with this group to garner more than $17 million in grant funds and has presented at the state and national levels on preparing teachers to succeed in high-need schools and assuring opportunity and access for the historically underrepresented students. Jan serves on and leads state task force groups to advance practice and policy for high-quality programs for all, publishes a biannual online journal, and leads an online professional development network for teachers and leaders. Jan has been a special education teacher, curriculum coordinator, and principal. Jan earned her PhD at the University of Chicago in education curriculum and instruction. This marks Jan's second book on teacher leadership and is a companion text to Rowman & Littlefield's *Identifying and Growing Internal Leaders: A Framework for Effective Teacher Leadership* (2019).

Debra K. Meyer, PhD is a professor of education and the Genevieve Staudt Endowed Chair at Elmhurst College. She was an elementary teacher in Mesa, Arizona, before earning a doctorate from The University of Texas–Austin in educational psychology. She teaches graduate courses in teacher leadership and action research as well as undergraduate courses for preservice teachers. Her research has examined the relationships among student and teacher motivations, emotions, teaching, and learning, and the professional transitions from preservice to in-service teacher. Currently she is working on projects investigating the development of teacher leadership through her endowed chair and the creation of a virtual Institute for Teacher Leadership. She has presented at national and international conferences and authored over forty publications. She is an editorial board member of the *American Education Research Journal*, *Journal of Experimental Education*, and *Theory into Practice*. She was an editor of a five-volume research to practice series, Classroom Insights from Educational Psychology, a joint publication of APA Division 15 with Corwin. She has received awards for teaching, advising, and professional service and holds memberships in Phi Kappa Phi, Kappa Delta Phi, and Omicron Delta Kappa honor societies.